YOU
ARE A
CHANNEL

ALSO BY SARA LANDON

The Wisdom of The Council

The Dream, the Journey, Eternity, and God, with Mike Dooley

All of the above are available at your local bookstore,
or may be ordered by visiting:

Hay House USA: www.hayhouse.com®
Hay House Australia: www.hayhouse.com.au
Hay House UK: www.hayhouse.co.uk
Hay House India: www.hayhouse.co.in

***

YOU
ARE A
CHANNEL

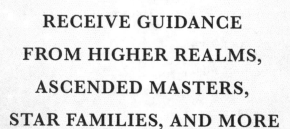

RECEIVE GUIDANCE
FROM HIGHER REALMS,
ASCENDED MASTERS,
STAR FAMILIES, AND MORE

SARA LANDON

HAY HOUSE LLC

Carlsbad, California • New York City
London • Sydney • New Delhi

Published in the United States by: Hay House LLC: www.hayhouse.com®
Published in Australia by: Hay House Australia Publishing Pty Ltd: www
.hayhouse.com.au • *Published in the United Kingdom by:* Hay House UK Ltd:
www.hayhouse.co.uk • *Published in India by:* Hay House Publishers (India)
Pvt Ltd: www.hayhouse.co.in

Cover design: Faceout Studios • *Interior design:* Nick C. Welch

Cataloging-in-Publication is on file with the Library of Congress.

Tradepaper ISBN: 978-1-4019-7676-7
E-book ISBN: 978-1-4019-7677-4
Audiobook ISBN: 978-1-4019-7678-1

10 9 8 7 6 5 4 3 2 1
1st edition, July 2024

Printed in the United States of America

SUSTAINABLE FORESTRY INITIATIVE
Certified Chain of Custody
Promoting Sustainable Forestry
www.forests.org
SFI-01268
SFI label applies to the text stock

This product uses responsibly sourced papers and/or recycled materials.
For more information, see www.hayhouse.com.

Dedicated to all who are ready to reconnect with their soul, higher self, guides, angels, and loved ones on the other side.

CONTENTS

INTRODUCTION

"While I have realized the potential that millions of people around the world will now be able to use The Council's wisdom to transform their lives and live their own highest potential, it's my deepest desire to leave a legacy where all those who are ready will discover their own ability to channel Source and access the grander perspective that is here for us all."

— Sara Landon

Who wouldn't want to communicate with their angels, guides, and loved ones on the other side? In this book, you will discover how you—*yes, you*—can access higher wisdom and receive guidance from your soul, spirit, guides, and soul team! I believe everyone has the ability to tune in to higher wisdom and connect into the infinite field of consciousness within us and all around us in every moment. Whether your desire is to communicate with your higher self, a loved one on the other side, or the collective consciousness of your guides, I assure you, it is possible for you, and this book will show you how.

When I started channeling, I did not have anyone who could explain to me what was going on. I thought I was going crazy, although I knew I wasn't. I thought I was making it up, but the truth and love I was channeling was undeniable. At times, this journey has been very difficult. I created a lot of stress and overwhelm for myself by doubting myself, holding back, and going into fear. It is my intention that your journey is easier, more harmonious, and much more fun than mine was in the beginning.

This book contains the information I wish I had possessed when I began my channeling journey so many years ago. It will guide you through the best practices that I have discovered, from my first conscious experience of communicating with higher wisdom in 1999 to my current professional career of channeling The Council for thousands of people all over the world. Anyone can do this. It is not a power that only a few have; it is a natural and inherent ability that we never intended to forget.

You Are a Channel also includes experiential processes and visualizations to assist you in opening and developing your own connection to infinite intelligence. Designed specifically for this book, you will also receive uplifting channeled messages from The Council to activate your true power and elevate your awareness. If you are drawn to channeled information or channeling in any form, you are simply reconnecting with the knowing of your own higher wisdom and consciousness.

Some years ago, I was inspired to begin teaching others how to communicate with higher levels of consciousness. To date, I have taught more than 5,000 people around the world how to channel. In this book, I will also share with you the inspiring stories of many of my students and their extraordinary experiences when learning to channel.

You are a channel; that's not a question. You all are a conduit, a vessel, a channel for divine love and divine light in the world. Everyone expresses this uniquely and differently. And everyone's journey is unique and different.

Once you have established your connection to Source Energy, a whole new and amazing world will begin to present itself to you, allowing you to discover your unique gifts, abilities, and talents. Your soul and your guides are inviting you to play in new realms of pure potential where higher wisdom is available to everyone. You might just meet your favorite Ascended Master or Archangel, only to realize they have been eagerly waiting to guide you and assist you on this magnificent adventure.

Trust the process, be gentle on yourself, and have fun with this! Everyone has an innate inherent ability to connect into higher consciousness, infinite potential, and Source Energy. This book is intended to guide you to remember a gift that is already within you, an ability that we all have but might have just forgotten.

I hope your channeling journey changes your life in the most extraordinary ways possible, as it has my own. Each of us is a channel of higher wisdom. I believe now more than ever, your light and love are needed in the world.

LIVING THE WISDOM: MY JOURNEY

"Live this wisdom, and you will have a life beyond your wildest dreams."

— The Council

I never desired to be a channel, but now I can't imagine my life any other way. I grew up in a loving Christian family in a small town. My family was Lutheran, and we attended church every Sunday and on holidays. I recall that I had a love for God and an awareness of my spiritual connection from a young age. When I was seven years old, my parents divorced. My mother and I moved out of state, closer to her family, including her sister, Sunnie.

From the moment I first met my Aunt Sunnie, I remember being fascinated by her. She spoke about the soul, the power of the mind, metaphysics, the supernatural, and her master teacher, Mafu. Sunnie would explain that Mafu was a highly evolved being that was channeled through a young woman named Penny. She would tell me stories for hours about her recollections of past lives, soulmates, miracles, and the teachings of Mafu.

I first heard Mafu speak while watching a video with Sunnie. I was instantly captivated. There was an electrifying connection to the voice and the words that were spoken. It was as if Mafu's words were something that I knew, and I felt a resonant buzzing throughout my body.

I can also remember how devastated I felt the first time I overheard my family poking fun at my aunt for believing *that stuff.* "How fake and phony," they would say. On one occasion, when I was about 10 years old, I remember a close family member saying to me, "If she believes in that stuff, she will go to hell—and so will you, if you believe it."

It severed a cord deep within my heart. How could they say that about her? And what kind of God would do that? That day, I felt the light within me go out.

Over the years, I continued to listen to Mafu's audio and video tapes and read books about spirituality, past lives, and other metaphysical teachings. Yet after that day, I rarely ever spoke about it to anyone but my aunt. I could not believe that the loving God I had sung about for all those years would damn someone like my aunt—or me—to hell.

On another occasion, I remember being told that people who do not accept Jesus in their hearts were going to hell. I asked, "What about people in Indigenous tribes or remote places in the world who've never heard of Jesus? Are they going to hell?" To which I was told, "Yes, that's what the Bible says."

Conflicted and overwhelmed by the contradiction between these ideas and what I was taught originally about a loving God, I lost interest in religion. I soon discovered personal development and cultivated a passion for achievement and life success. My focus became setting goals, starting my career, and climbing the corporate ladder. I was driven by the desire to succeed and build a prosperous life.

Yet I would continually find myself reading books on spirituality and metaphysics. I was still searching for answers about life, God, Heaven and hell, truth, and the meaning of it all. Many years went by during which I considered myself an atheist despite knowing there was more to life than just living and dying.

That is, until one blistering cold wintry day in November 2001—a day that would forever change the course of my life. I remember the heaviness in the room as I walked in to view the body of my deceased brother, Tim. He had been killed in a car accident the previous day. My family and I had flown to Alaska where he had been living. I had never seen a dead body, nor could I wrap my brain around my brother being gone. As I touched him, I was shocked by the cold, hard texture of his lifeless body. I immediately wanted to get away and made my way over to a chair on the far side of the room.

I felt numb as I sat listening to the quiet sobbing of my mother and other family members. I can't tell you exactly how long I sat there. It felt like hours, but I am sure it was only minutes. Suddenly and unexpectedly, I felt this sense of peace wash over me. I began to feel a warm sensation of energy—like liquid love—flowing down from the crown of my head and into my entire body. I was completely and totally at peace and surrounded by a sense of love.

Then over my right shoulder I heard my brother say to me, *"I am still here. I am just not in there,"* referring to his body. In my mind, I replied, *"Where are you?"* He replied, *"I am just as here as I ever was. I just left the density of the body. I am at a frequency that your physical senses cannot interpret,"* he said.

Although his words seemed strange, I understood. My immediate next question was, *"Are you in Heaven?"* To which he replied, *"Heaven and hell aren't like that. They are only experiences one has on Earth. There is only love here."*

Then as spontaneously as it began, the energy receded, and the communication stopped. I was back in the cold room. Looking around at my family, I was sure that no one except me had heard Tim. In that moment I felt absolute peace about my brother's death, yet longed to speak with him again.

I didn't tell anyone about the conversation. Within a few days, I started to doubt that it had really happened and began to question whether I had made it all up. But I could not deny what I felt or forget what he said.

Again and again, I attempted to reconnect to my brother and summon that warm liquid-love feeling. For many weeks, nothing happened. Then one day, as I was walking into the elevator at my office on the way back from lunch, I started to feel warm all over, and my hands began to tingle. There was no one in the elevator but me and a man I had never seen before. Over my right shoulder, I heard my brother say, *"Ask him his name."*

"I am not asking him his name," I responded mentally. But he persisted and again told me to ask the man his name. Feeling a bit ridiculous, but doing as Tim said, I asked the man his name. "Tim," he said, and then casually walked out the open doors of the elevator. Tim is my brother's name, I thought! This *is* real!

These types of experiences continued for years. My brother would spontaneously drop in with a message over my right shoulder. It was always preceded by a deep feeling of peace and love, and I soon began to know when he was there. I didn't know at the time (as I do now) how to connect with him intentionally or deliberately, but I felt comforted to know he was with me.

Some years later, at the height of my professional career, I started having strange experiences in the middle of the night. I would wake up and feel consumed by the desire to write. I had no memory of what I was writing and no idea from where the writing came. In the morning, I would read what I'd written. It was certainly not information that I knew, and it wasn't written in the way that I usually spoke. The handwriting was noticeably different than my own. It contained the answers to my deepest questions about life, existence, God, and the universe. The writing was so beautiful, so loving, so wise. I couldn't summon the writing on command, but it continued spontaneously for several months. I now know this is an experience referred to as *automatic writing.*

Other strange things started to happen. I would look at a clock as it would read 1:11, 11:11, 2:22, 3:33, 4:44, 5:55. I started finding feathers when out on walks. I began to feel a deep love for flowers, birds, and animals. For seemingly no apparent reason, I would become overwhelmed with feelings of blissfulness and love. I felt one with everything and everyone and would often know what people were going to say before they said it. I would begin to think of a friend or loved one, and within minutes, they would call.

And while I felt such love and oneness, I would equally and as strongly feel a deep sense of sadness about the human experience and the suffering in the world. One moment I was immersed in love, peace, joy, and oneness, and the next minute I felt hopeless and lost. It was as if I had the wisdom of the world within me but no idea about my purpose or how to live it.

Several months later, I met a woman in hot yoga. I had noticed her in class a couple of days in a row. On the third day, I introduced myself. I asked her how she liked yoga and she replied, "I had to give it a try, but I am never coming back."

I laughed, not surprised, and asked her what she did. She explained she was a practitioner of Quantum Healing Hypnosis Technique. "What?" I asked. She explained that she helped people communicate with their higher selves and connect to information from the other side. Intrigued, and hoping she could help me figure out what was going on in my life, I scheduled a session with her.

A few days later, she came to my house for the QHHT session. She led me through a guided meditation and then asked, "Do we have permission to talk with Sara's higher self?" I said, "Yes," and she began to ask questions. We continued until suddenly my entire body was flooded with energy even beyond the warm liquid love. It was like nothing I had ever felt. It was like being shocked with volts of love, bliss, and ecstasy.

My hands and feet were tingling, and I felt a lightness—as if I was floating. My voice began to change, and I noticed that I had an accent and was speaking very quickly. I would later describe it like the voice of an Eastern European man. The peculiar voice coming through me went on speaking for over an hour. I was aware of myself but also aware that it wasn't *me* talking. I didn't remember what was said, but I could feel the truth and love in the words that were coming through. Luckily, the session had been recorded.

Afterward, I felt amazing. I could barely sleep that night. I was so energized and eager to replay the recording. As I listened to the peculiar voice, I realized the information being spoken was the same as that which had been coming through in my writings months before. I was intrigued and excited, but also determined that no one would ever hear the replay of me talking in that strange voice.

The knowledge contained in the recording, however, was so profound that I just had to have another QHHT session. Again, the peculiar voice came through, only this time I was present for the entire conversation. Although I couldn't clearly remember everything, I was aware of what the voice was saying. On many occasions, the voice referred to itself as *we* or *us*.

Over time we began to call the voice The Council, as it seemed to be a group of wise, old souls providing answers to our many questions, thereby expanding our awareness. We continued with weekly sessions. Each time, more of my consciousness was present to the conversation. Eventually, I was fully aware of the information that was coming through me from The Council. Their messages felt like the deepest truth I had ever known, and as if I were remembering something I already knew.

THE COUNCIL'S FOUNDATIONAL TEACHINGS

The wisdom of The Council and its impact is multifaceted. Their unique perspective, their sometimes unusual way of saying things, and their obvious love for us affects us in many ways. Those of us compelled by their wisdom, however, find the *truths* they bring forward to be the most impactful when used as a guide to living well. These truths include:

- You are already everything you wish to be.

- You are the Creator within your own creation of reality.

- Life is meant to be joyful.

- What you focus on and the meaning you give it is what creates your reality.

- Consciousness moves energy into form; this is the formula for all creation.

- There is only love.

- Everything is always happening *for* you, not *to* you.

- You are Source Energy that *you* focused into a physical body.

- If you want to experience anything in the world around you, you must first create it within yourself.

- You have everything you need within you—and an infinite supply of resources—to create the life of your dreams.

- You have come here by your own choosing from an expanded state of consciousness to experience life (energy) in physical form.

- Life is a grand adventure, and the journey only continues on from here.

- All of your power is in the now moment.

- Stillness is the access point to acceleration.

- There is no need to make big decisions about anything; allow all things to be *choiceless*.

- As you align to a higher level of consciousness, your well-being and abundance are assured.

- True Creation has no agenda.

- You get more of what you *are*, not what you *want*. If you want more joy in your life, align to the joy that is already within you and around you.

- When you are resisting anything, you are resisting everything and stopping the flow of easy, effortless, harmonious creation.

I had an absolute knowing of these truths when I first heard them despite having no idea how to live them. While each session with The Council always felt so pure, blissful, and loving, in my mind I could hear the words of my Christian family telling me that I would go to hell if I believed this stuff. I kept hearing all the things they said about my Aunt Sunnie and Penny, the woman who channeled Mafu. I now imagined them saying those things about me. More than anything, I feared losing the love and admiration of my dad. I just knew he would not understand.

For almost a year, I continued doing sessions but told almost no one of The Council. We recorded hundreds of hours of information. I had the recordings transcribed and would read and reread every session. The wisdom and teachings were positively transforming every aspect of my life. Still, I had no idea what to do with all the information.

My only desire was to consume The Council's wisdom, walk my dogs, and spend time in nature. By this point, and to the shock of almost all my friends, family, and co-workers, I had resigned from my flourishing corporate career. I began meditating daily and within minutes could feel The Council's love and my consciousness merging with theirs. However, I want to emphasize that I never experience The Council as outside of me or as if they are taking me over. My connection with The Council occurs because I connect to a frequency *within* me that allows me to expand my awareness into higher levels of consciousness, which have always been there and available to me.

As time went on, I began spending hours translating the streams of thought that I was receiving daily through my connection to them. After some months of writing, I started recording voice communications. I had no idea why I was doing this, but I just trusted it, because it felt like what I was meant to do.

I had no plans to ever tell anyone about The Council. I didn't want people to think I was weird or woo-woo, but at the same time, I knew that I had to get The Council's powerful teachings to others and allow them to experience the transformation for themselves. Despite my trepidation, I offered sessions to a couple of close friends. Those sessions were profound and moving. They began to describe their experience as a feeling of coming home, the gift of a lifetime, and the truth they had been searching for their entire lives. Each person I shared The Council with began to experience rapid and miraculous transformations and manifestations in their lives. Within a few short years, I was doing sessions with The Council for people all over the world by phone.

The wisdom of The Council has now expanded into courses, books, seminars, summits, retreats, and a global community of people living The Council's wisdom and teachings. And I live a life *beyond* my wildest dreams, just as they assured me I would. Since channeling and integrating The Council's wisdom, my life has more love, joy, abundance, freedom, well-being, and harmony than I ever thought possible.

I also now understand the original intention of the teachings of the Bible and the Christian religion. My own personal relationship with Jesus is one of love, appreciation, and continual presence in my life. I believe Jesus to be a great master whose wisdom came from the same origin and consciousness as that of The Council.

What's more, my greatest fear never materialized; my family has supported me in miraculous ways, and many now listen to The Council daily. My relationship with my dad is more loving and meaningful than ever before. He even shared with me that he had the same experience as I did with Tim when his father passed away. The night of my grandfather's death, my dad was lying in bed when suddenly he felt total peace and heard my grandfather say, *"Be in peace. All is well. I am here."* My father told me in that moment he was relieved of all his grief and sadness.

My desire to discover my truth, my purpose, and the meaning of life is what summoned the consciousness of The Council. If you are reading this now, I can say the same for you. You drew this book to you at just the perfect time. You, too, are a channel of Divine Love and higher wisdom—a part of The Council on Earth.

I've dedicated countless hours to channeling The Council's wisdom and sharing their messages to all who are ready to receive them. These are my deepest, heartfelt wishes for you:

May you remember the infinite wisdom that lies within you.

May you reconnect with the light that you are.

May you realize yourself as a powerful extension of Source Energy.

I have devoted my life to living The Council's profound, life-changing wisdom each and every day. I welcome you to join me on this incredible journey of channeling. This book is potentially my greatest gift to the world, and creating it for you has been the joy of a lifetime.

A MESSAGE FROM THE COUNCIL ON CHANNELING

We are so pleased and delighted to have the opportunity to speak with you on this fine and glorious day indeed. You are everything you wish to be; you already are. You are a vessel and conduit of Source Energy and divine love and truth in the world. You are a channel of infinite intelligence, infinite love, infinite well-being, and infinite abundance.

You are either cutting off your channel, slowing it down, limiting divine love, or you are opening and expanding it, and fully allowing it, which is what you intended as the extension of Source Energy that is you when you focused yourself into this human experience. What you call channeling—discovering the channel that you already are—it's about consciously, intentionally opening and allowing all that is here for you and available for you in every moment.

You have this. You are this. You can do this. You can *have it all* in your life. When you say I want to have it all, what you're really saying is, "I want to fully open my channel to the infinite love and infinite well-being and infinite abundance and infinite intelligence that is the divine inherent birthright that I knew I had when I chose to come into this magnificent life experience." You just learned to limit it or doubt it or deny it or not trust all that is here for you.

Go outside and find something beautiful, or go pet your dog or your cat, or be with your family and intentionally, consciously feel the love and the beauty and the appreciation. If you are looking at a beautiful flower, really focus on that flower. Then open and allow Source to see that beautiful flower through your eyes, to smell that beautiful flower through your nose. As you're gazing upon someone you love, open and allow all of Source to feel the love that you're feeling, and you will begin to open your channel and your awareness.

Trust your channel, and you learn to allow it in a way that you can tune in to this connection to Source at any time and expand it. It becomes your way of being and how you live your life. You will notice that gifts, abilities, and talents begin to present themselves to you.

You have known that there was more to you. You have known that you had a greater calling or higher potential, even if you did not know what it was. In opening fully and allowing the Source Energy that is always available to you, you will begin to channel to you all that is you!

We in higher levels of consciousness have never been separate from you. However, you have free will. That is how powerful you are. You can doubt your connection and deny it if it is your choosing, but we think once you fully experience it for yourself, you will *know* that it is who you really are and how you intended your life to be.

You are everything you wish to be. You already are. It is all within you and it always has been. Come into embodying the enlightened master of you that you are so that you can live fully and love fully and be all that you are on the planet at this time. That is the *most* important thing. We are always with you. We are always available to you. We love you, we love you, we love you. And with that, we are complete.

CHAPTER 1

WHY CHANNELING, WHY NOW

You might be asking yourself why you have suddenly been drawn to a book on channeling or why you have started to have channeled experiences of your own. You might be newly awakened, or maybe you have been on a spiritual path for many years now. Regardless of where you are on your journey, there is a reason you have been guided to channeling and to reading this book. You have a greater calling, and now is the time to discover it, live it, and create the magnificent life that you are here to experience!

Many people believe channeling is an otherworldly mystical experience where one hears the booming voice of God or sees angels come down from the sky appearing in front of them. For most of us, that is not the experience we have. Channeling is often far more subtle than you think—presenting as the still, quiet voice within. Because of that, people sometimes disregard channeled experiences or believe they are making it up in their head. When people do not have someone to share their experiences with, they often feel alone and isolated.

Until now, channeling was not typically discussed in everyday walks of life or social circles. However, that is no longer the case. Channeling is being demystified and becoming far more common and approachable in everyday life. Movie scripts, actors, athletes, musicians, and celebrities are often quoted as saying, "I was channeling Babe Ruth when I hit that home run." Or you might hear a musician say, "I was channeling Mozart when I played that piece."

In fact, I recently heard a friend who is not a channel herself say, "I must have been channeling my grandmother when I was making that pie. My pie crust never turns out this good."

Channeling is natural, normal, and far more available to us than most people think. Although we often refer to our soul, angels, and guides as beings in higher consciousness that appear to be *up there* or *out there*, they really are right here within you as you expand your awareness and field of consciousness. Channeling is the act of connecting, communicating, and communing with Divine wisdom and Source Energy. This connection has the potential to profoundly and positively uplevel your life. The result is that you will begin to experience more love, joy, peace, well-being, freedom, fulfillment, abundance, beauty, and prosperity in every area of your life.

Channeling is so much more than just asking questions. It is a shift in your perception and perspective. It is an elevation of one's vibration, consciousness, and awareness to connect into a force field of infinite intelligence all around you. And it is always available to everyone who desires to reach for higher wisdom and a grander perspective on their truth and their experience. Channeling is quite possibly the greatest tool available for personal and spiritual transformation.

If you look back at your life experience, you might feel that you have been preparing for something, been initiated to some greater mission in this life, or feel determined to discover your purpose. While I had a successful career as a corporate executive, I always felt like there was some bigger purpose in my life. Yet I had no idea what that was or even where to begin in order to discover it.

I had a deep fascination with how one lives their highest potential in life. While I had no desire to be a channel, I was drawn to channeled information such that I did not resonate with any material that was not a result of channeled wisdom. I was seeking answers on how to live my purpose, as well as the answers to life's biggest, deepest questions.

Not only did I receive the answers to all of those questions and more, but the consciousness, vibration, and awareness that accompanied those channeled answers brought me into an experience of realization. What is realization? To me, it's the realization of Heaven on Earth, a New Earth, the Promised Land, a state of pure love, and complete freedom.

I also realized that every step of the way, some greater power and higher intelligence was guiding me, placing the next perfect step in front of me, and orchestrating divine appointments for everyone I was destined to meet along my path. Once I began channeling The Council, I not only understood that my entire life was preparing me for it, but why I was being prepared for *this time* on our planet.

You are entering into the most powerful time of your life. You are no longer preparing. You are no longer an initiate. You are a master. *Now is the time. This is what you've been waiting for and preparing for likely your entire life.* This is what you came for and this is why you are *here*. You are needed now more than ever to be all that you are and to live your life fully and to love fully. Let me expound.

The Council explains that we are in the time of the Great Awakening, the greatest transformation of human consciousness that has ever existed in any lifetime. You have chosen to be on the planet at this time, to awaken yourself, and then simply be the divine love that you are, while also being a shining light for others along the way. You are a wayshower, to show that more is possible for all of humankind. There is a potential for all of humanity to live in a fully awakened world, a New Earth experience where there is peace, joy, love, harmony, freedom, and abundance for all. You are the bridge to this new world.

This time now is bringing forth the greatest, most expansive wave of awakening of humanity that has ever occurred. You're going to see the Great Awakening unfolding all around you. You're going to see it in your friendships, in your relationships, in your co-workers, with strangers, and even in the people that you likely doubted would ever awaken. They are awakening because of you, because you have raised the consciousness, because you raised the vibration, because you brought the light.

This is why you and so many people are feeling the call to something greater, to some greater purpose, and to some greater mission. This is why people are feeling such a strong desire to live their highest potential and to be who they are in the world. Maybe understanding what is going on *behind the scenes* of this time of the Great Awakening will help to make sense of some of what you have been feeling, the sense of urgency you might be feeling, the intensity that you might be feeling, or even the incredible momentum that you may be experiencing in your own life at this time.

It is not your responsibility to awaken everyone or save a broken world. It is not your responsibility to hypothetically throw everyone over your shoulder and carry them across the finish line or figure it out for them. It is your responsibility to live the Great Awakening for yourself and transform your own consciousness into pure love and complete freedom. It is about taking personal responsibility for every area of your life and every aspect of your creation. Only you can determine what taking personal responsibility for your life means to you. It is not a judgment of right or wrong. It is simply about being conscious and aware of how you are living your life and expressing your truth in the world around you.

So, why are you here? Why does it matter? What is your purpose? Continue to ask yourself these questions until you come into the realization of the deeper truth of you. You're here for a reason or you wouldn't be here. You have a purpose, and it's time for you to discover it and live it. I believe there is something deeper inside each one of us that knows there is a far greater purpose for Earth and its inhabitants in this vast and glorious universe. More people living an awakened life on Earth expands the potentials and the possibilities for all of humankind.

A Visualization to Answer the Big Questions

If you wish, record yourself reading the message below, then use the recording to help you deepen into the visualization.

Take some deep breaths. Allow your awareness to move from your head into your heart and feel your body relax. Remember that here is a part of you that knows who you are, where you are going, and what is truly possible for you. Become aware of not only your higher self but your future self. Tune your awareness now to your future self.

It might be the future self of you 5 years from now, or maybe 10 years from now. It is the future self of you who has lived fully and loved fully and had the experience of being all that you are. It is the part of you that already knows who you are here to become. It is the part of you that knows a new journey into higher dimensions of consciousness is beginning to present itself to you now.

Just notice which future self is presenting itself to you. What does your future self want to show you? What does your future self want to tell you about everything that you are going through now and everything you are about to go through? This part of you is already on the other side of it all and is in the realization of all that you are becoming. What does your future self want to tell you about why you are here? What does your future self want to tell you about your purpose and your highest potential?

What does your future self want you to know about who you are, why you're here, and what's really possible for you? Your future self is the part of you that knows you are perfect, whole, and complete in this. It is the wisest part of you, the most loving part of you standing at the finish line with their arms out wide, waiting for you to fall into their arms. They are holding you, telling you how proud they are of you, that you did such a good job, that they love you so much. "You did it," they might say. "And look, it wasn't as hard as you made it out to be. It really wasn't that scary. You did it."

Take a few moments and see if anything else comes to you from your wise, loving future self. Are there any other messages that your future self has for you? Remember, you can always go to this place and connect with your future self that already knows who you are to become and the easiest, most harmonious path of your journey to becoming everything you wish to be.

CHAPTER 2

WHAT YOUR SOUL WANTS YOU TO KNOW

Have you ever desired to receive direct communication from your soul, guides, or loved ones on the other side? Well, *you can!* You can access guidance and messages from your higher self or *anyone* at any time once you understand an easy, expansive process to find out exactly what messages await you.

Your soul has infinite wisdom and knowledge to share with you in this very moment that could instantly create greater peace, joy, abundance, well-being, and love in your life. Your connection to your soul is the source of intuition, inspiration, and imagination, and will guide you to the highest potential for your life. Your soul knows how you are, where you are, and the most effortless path to endless experiences of true creation and grand manifestation.

Not only can you discover what your own soul wants you to know, but you can also receive messages from the higher self of anyone. This process works whether that person is still alive, is on the other side, or is known or unknown personally to you. For example, you can communicate and receive guidance from the higher self of a great leader, teacher, or master who once lived on earth. Your higher self and the higher self of anyone is always available to communicate with you. You can also ask for messages from your angels, pets, other animals, or elements of nature.

When I first started channeling, The Council encouraged me to journal every morning. *"Journaling?"* I thought to myself, and you might be thinking this too: "I don't have time for journaling. I don't *like* journaling. I don't want to journal. I don't have anything to journal about. *I'm not doing that!"*

However, I will tell you that journaling, and more specifically, the automatic writing process I am going to share with you—which is, in and of itself, a form of channeling—has changed my life in countless, unimaginable ways. Over the years, my soul has consistently, without fail, come forth with a message to guide me to the highest perspective of a situation or offered words of inspiration and direction when I felt uncertain or unsure. Anytime I have any sort of question, concern, or issue in my life, I use this process to ask for a message from either my higher self, my guides, or someone else's higher self.

To begin the process, get some paper and something to write with. Have it nearby and easily available. Close your eyes and take three deep, conscious breaths. I emphasize that three breaths or more are an important part of the process. Then, move your awareness from your head down into your heart. Imagine a staircase beginning in your head and leading into your heart. Step down, step-by-step, from your head down into your heart. Once you get to your heart, imagine a door appearing in front of you that leads into your heart. Gently reach down, open the door, and walk into your heart. Take a few moments and be present, and feel how good it feels to be in your heart. You might notice that you feel calm and that the mind chatter is suddenly quiet. Feel the peace and serenity in your heart.

Then, with your eyes still closed, ask the question, "What does my soul most want me to know?" Or you might ask, "What does my higher self most want me to know?" Continue asking the question in whatever way feels good to you. You might simply ask, "What message does my soul have for me in this moment?"

When you are ready, open your eyes, and start writing whatever comes to you. Allow whatever messages you are hearing or thinking to flow through you onto your paper. Keep writing and don't worry about making sense of it or editing it. You might feel like you are making it up. That's quite normal. Keep going. Write until you feel the message is complete or you feel the energy recede. This might be a few words, a few sentences, a few pages or more. It's perfectly fine to stop and take some deep breaths and ask again, "What does my soul want me to know?" It doesn't matter how long or short the message is. You might even feel an abrupt end to the message, which is also a normal occurrence.

If nothing immediately comes to you, start writing the words, "I am so happy and grateful." Repeat, "I am so happy and grateful." Begin writing down the things you are happy and grateful for. You might write, "I am so happy and grateful for my life, my family, my pets, my job."

Focus on writing down all the things you are grateful for. Before long, you might notice that something shifts and a message begins to come through to you. Allow it to flow through you from that state of feeling happy and grateful.

When doing this process, you can use whatever words feel good to you. What does my soul want me to know? What does my soul want me to know today? What does Source want me to know today? If you have an angel or loved one on the other side, you can say their name specifically and ask, "What' do *you* most want me to know?" Do what feels good to you each day as you do your automatic writing and know that there is no wrong way.

Remember, sometimes it's three words or three sentences. Sometimes it's three pages. Sometimes it's three minutes and other times it's 30 minutes. The length is not important. It's also very common to notice that your handwriting or penmanship changes. It's very common for the punctuation to be unusual. It's very common that the message might appear to come from a collective and use the phrase "we" or "us." For example, "we love you, we're here for you, we see you."

You might feel like you're making it up. You might feel like nothing's happening, but trust the process and create the space to do it consistently, preferably each day. Think of it as your sacred time to connect with Source or spirit. Don't make it a job. You might want to turn on music, light a candle, or find a quiet place out in nature to do this process.

You might notice that the message is repetitive day after day until you *get the message.* You might wonder why you get the same message, but it's exactly the message you most need to hear regardless of how simple it might appear. Don't judge the message, just write. Once you *get the message,* new messages will come or the guidance will expand.

Now, here is a critical and important part of the automatic writing process. When you get through journaling, either read the message back to yourself *out loud,* have someone else read it back to you out loud, or read it out loud to someone you feel comfortable with. In my experience, this is crucial. You will quickly begin to feel the energy and power in the message when it's read out loud.

When you are writing, you are hearing the message in your head, in the same voice from which you wrote the message. However, when you read it out loud or have someone read it back to you, you will feel the energy and power of the message differently than the voice in your head. You might even notice strong, loving emotions that arise within you as you hear the message read out loud.

For most people, handwriting your messages is preferrable. However, some people like to type the messages out on their computer. That's perfectly fine. Others like to use the voice memos in their phone or a recording device to speak out loud what's coming to them.

Again, there is no wrong way to do this. The most important thing is to trust yourself and open up to the guidance and wisdom you are receiving. I cannot emphasize enough that *you are going to feel like you are making it up,* but even if you are, keep going.

Prior to teaching groups of people about the art of channeling, I would take people through a one-on-one experience to open to their own channel. I remember a wonderful woman from Germany I worked with who was eager to learn how to channel. I asked her to do the journaling exercise and commit to the automatic writing practice each day. After about a week, she said, "I just don't think anything is happening." I asked her to e-mail me a photo of what she had written. She sent it to me, and during her next session, I read the messages out loud to her.

They sounded like this, "We want you to know that we are always with you and you are never alone. You are exactly where you are meant to be. There are great things coming for you. There's nothing you need to figure out. You are worthy of all the goodness. You are so loved, so cared for, so guided in every moment. Everything will come together perfectly in divine right time."

As I was reading the messages out loud to her, I could tell she was crying and had become very emotional as I read on. There is just *something* that happens when you hear the messages out loud for yourself. She said, "Oh my gosh, I really thought I was making it up, but that's so beautiful. I never could have come up with anything like that."

It's normal to think you are making it up and that the message is coming from your head and not from your soul or spirit. However, consider what the voice in your head might *really* sound like. It might say something like this: "You should be doing *this*. You should have gotten *that* done. You should do *this* today. You should figure *that* out. You haven't gotten *this* done yet. You should do more of *this*. You shouldn't have said *that*. You should say *that* and go do *this*. You messed *that* up. You missed out on *that*." That's what the voice in our heads usually sounds like. It's usually not the loving, comforting, supporting, all-knowing voice of understanding and kindness.

Over many years of teaching people from all over the world how to channel, I have read and heard thousands of messages from people's souls, higher selves, guides, and loved ones. The messages all carry a similar emphasis on love, acceptance, understanding, peace, and encouragement. They never judge. They never condemn. They often sound similar because Source, no matter what vessel it's coming through, *is love,* is unconditional love, is unwavering love, knows the truth of you, knows that it's all perfect, knows that there's divine orchestration happening at all times. If you get the same message time and time again, it's because your soul and guides are sincerely inviting you to *embody it.* Your soul is *really trying* to get that message to you. You might also notice, as it is common, to have messages about self-love, loving yourself more, self-worth, and feeling a sense of worthiness.

Worthiness and self-love are the doorway to your infinite self, your true self beyond your physical form, who has always existed and will always exist. Spirit continuously encourages you to know you are worthy of the infinite intelligence that's available to you in every moment, that anyone's higher self, no matter where they are, is available to you, that your higher self is always out ahead of you orchestrating things on your path, to know that you are worthy and you matter *that much,* and you're *that loved.* When you can truly allow *that,* you will live in this ever-present flow of divine love, a divine state of being, and everything in your life will absolutely go to another level of peace, joy, love, harmony, abundance, well-being, freedom. Everything!

You will notice that everything begins to change in the most positive and empowering ways: your physical body, relationships, mindset, sense of well-being, level of abundance, your whole life. Since I began channeling, everything in my life has transformed beyond my wildest dreams, beyond what I could have ever thought to ask for myself. This kind of transformation is a natural result of opening to channeling, and *it's possible for everyone.* It changes how to think, act, feel, respond, and therefore changes your entire life.

Early on in my relationship with my partner, I felt hurt by a situation that had arisen between us. Prior to being aware of this powerful technique to communicate with his higher self, I would have gotten upset, been triggered, reacted, and it would have likely led to an argument. Instead, I turned to this process. I went into my office, sat down, took some deep breaths, went into my heart. I thought of a time when I felt deep love between us and began to feel the presence of his higher self around me. I said, "What does your soul want me to know?" And instantly, I started writing.

Did I think as I was writing that I was *making it up?* Yeah, I did. I thought I was making it up and writing what I thought he would say. I set the doubt aside and just kept writing. The message went on for several pages. After it stopped, I read the message back to myself out loud. I was in tears as I felt the love of his higher self pouring through the pages. I felt loved and peaceful. My awareness had been shifted into a place of acceptance and understanding. My heart was so full of love. The feelings of hurt were gone and did not arise again.

A few weeks later I told him about the message I had received that day from his higher self. I asked if he wanted to hear it, and he said he would. I read it to him and almost immediately tears welled up in his eyes. Once I finished, he told me, "I couldn't have said it any better myself. That's exactly what I wanted to say to you."

You can use this powerful process in your relationships with anyone: a spouse, significant other, child, parent, relative, friend, co-worker, boss. Instead of responding with a triggered wounded reaction, you can use this process to heal yourself. You will heal yourself, your relationships, and just maybe, begin to heal the world around you.

One of my students, a woman from California, explains her experience of connecting with her loved one's higher self. "The most impactful thing I received from working with Sara was the gift of channeling my 15-year-old daughter, who was born with a very rare genetic condition called KCNQ2 epileptic encephalopathy. She is disabled, in a wheelchair, fed through a tube in her stomach, and is nonverbal. I have always known and experienced her as much more than her physical presence. She is such a happy, positive, social person. Even though she can't move or speak, she can make a complete stranger's day with her energy and her smile.

"The first time I channeled her, she said, 'Hi Mommy. I love you.' I had waited 15 years to hear those words! Now, not only can I connect to her at any moment through the love we share, and feel it flow through me as her energy, she says 'I love you' all the time now, and expresses her love and appreciation of me in so many ways when I channel her. It is deeply fulfilling to be able to communicate with her in this way.

"Channeling my daughter has validated what a part of me already knew—that she was much more than her physical body—*that we all are!* I have become more aware of her higher truth, and more able to bring this perspective into my everyday life with her. Through this relationship with her, I feel more peace, more joy, and I don't get stuck in lower dimensions of consciousness or defeating thought patterns.

"I have moved beyond fear of the unknown, questions of why our life is the way it is, as well as the jealousy around not having a *normal* life. I have more energy to enjoy every precious moment with her, and live our life to the fullest. Channeling her has ultimately shown me our higher purpose in this life. We are excited to share our journey so that others on a similar path may find the same joy, peace, and healing that we have, and be able to more fully experience life with their children."

As you get comfortable with this process, you might discover that messages begin to come through you for other people. You might question what someone will think of you if you tell them you received a message for them. For example, from a loved one on the other side. There are several ways to gently approach this and determine whether the other person is open to receive the message.

You might simply say, "I was journaling recently and received a message that I feel is for you. Is it okay if I share it with you?" Most of the time, they will say yes. If not, don't take it personally. They are not ready to hear it now and might never be. However, in most cases, people are open and eager to receive a message of hope and love.

When you share a message from someone's higher self, there are ways to make it approachable and gentle. I recently read a message I received from someone's higher self during the eulogy at their celebration of life. I began by saying, "I think if she/he were here, this might be what they would want to say to us." There are many approaches to sharing a message you receive in a way that feels open and inviting to others. It's all about how you deliver it.

I had another aha moment when I worked with a lovely woman from Wisconsin. She was doing the journaling exercise daily. Yet the only person she had to share it with was her husband, and he was not familiar with automatic writing. She would start the conversation like this: "I know it's really weird, and I know you think I'm woo-woo, and I know it's totally crazy, but I got this message. I know it's totally weird, but do you want to hear it?" Not surprisingly when using this approach, he replied begrudgingly, "Well, okay, if I must."

After discussing with her how important it is to be gentle and approachable in your delivery, she began saying to her husband, "Wow, I got the most beautiful message today. I'm so excited about it! Oh, it just makes me so happy to read it. Can I share it with you?" This time he said, "Yes," without hesitation. He started coming to her every day and asking to hear her message from the day. *It's all in your delivery!*

I have a dear family member who is a devout Christian and only knows Spirit as Jesus or God. She is not familiar with channeling or higher-self communication. Some years ago, her beloved dog passed away in what many would consider a tragic accident. As soon as I heard the news of her dog, I got my journal, sat down, and asked for a message from her dog. The message was so beautiful, but there were some things in the message that were very specific and unusual to me. I wondered again if I was making it up and thought that it might be overwhelming to share the message with her. I contemplated it for a while, but finally felt clear that I was to share it with her. I called her and said, "I asked God if He would share a message with me about your dog. I got a message from your dog. Is it okay if I share it with you?" Enthusiastically, she said, "Oh, yes, please do!"

I read it to her and immediately she started to cry. When I finished, she thanked me numerous times. She then went immediately to the two specific things that I thought I was completely making up and seemed so random to me. One of those things was that her dog said that he was *doing this* to protect her. He said, "I left to protect you." She said, "I got chills when you read that part and felt so moved." She went on to tell me those were exactly the words—verbatim—that came to her about the tragic accident and the way her dog transitioned. She went on and on thanking me for the message and sharing her appreciation for the comfort she felt.

You never know what's going to happen with this process and what messages might come through *out of the blue.* Some have even compared this process to having the archangels and ascended masters on speed dial. I will share much more about that in later chapters, but if you feel the presence of an angel, archangel, or ascended master, known or unknown to you, just know that is a very normal experience when using this process. Trust it, trust yourself, have fun with it!

This process is life-changing in so many ways. Recently, a dear friend passed away. When I received the news, I allowed myself to feel the emotion of it, knowing that what I was feeling behind the sadness and the grief I was experiencing in that moment, was love. In any moment, we can stay in an awareness of love and not create a belief and a separation that something you love *is gone*. I sat in the emotion I was feeling of my dear friend no longer being here in human form. Once the initial sadness passed, using this process, I asked my friend for a message from his higher self.

I begin to think of how much fun we had at a celebration for my birthday a few years prior. I saw him as healthy and happy. I could literally see the smile on his face, and then I could feel his higher self there with me. I began to write, and his message flowed through me. After almost five pages of information for me, his wife, his daughters, and our friends, he ended his message. I went back and read the message out loud. From that moment, I have not felt a single instance of sadness or grief about his transition. I *know* he's right here.

A few weeks later I shared my experience with his wife and daughters and asked if I could read his message to them. They were eager to hear it. Although it was emotional for them, they expressed what incredible peace and comfort they felt as the message had so clearly come directly from him.

I have done this with my grandparents, my pets, and many other loved ones that have transitioned. I have also used this process to connect with many people's higher self, and every single time, the message comes forth bringing an expanded awareness or consciousness that shifts me out of whatever perceived story I've got going on, into peace, joy, harmony, love, consciousness, and understanding.

This is one of the most powerful tools to open your own connection to channeling and receiving messages. The people that really apply themselves to this, trust the process, do the exercise, and journal frequently, experience the most amazing connection to higher wisdom. I encourage you to follow the process over the coming days and weeks, making time each morning, or whatever time of day feels good to you, or when you feel most aligned, to journal.

I also encourage you to find a buddy that you can share your messages with and have them read your messages back to you. This is an important part of the process that will help you learn to trust. Remember, have fun, and explore the endless possibilities that become available to you as you open to receive messages from your soul and infinite intelligence.

A Message from The Council on Opening and Allowing

We are so pleased and delighted to have the opportunity to speak with you on this fine and glorious day indeed. We remind you that while our words to you are important, this is a vibrational experience of allowing yourself into the truth of all that you are, so that you can remember why you are here and all that you intended when you chose this magnificent life experience.

You have taken this human experience far too seriously for far too long; it is time for you to fully open up to the levels of consciousness that are available to you and that will reveal to you your gifts, your abilities, and your sacred knowledge.

Your human experiences from lower dimensions of consciousness prevent you from being in the energy, the creation energy that *you are* and that you come from. You haven't even begun to realize all that you are and all that is possible for you. Even the biggest dream in your heart is barely scratching the surface of the life that you are experiencing now in higher levels of consciousness.

When you come into the realization of all that you are through allowing your vibration to raise your level of consciousness, you begin to open up to everything that has been here for you all along. Life gets easier. It's so much more fun. You play and create in new levels of potential and possibility. You draw to you extraordinary collaborations, co-creations, and community with what you might call your soul group or your soulmates. They are all around this planet having this experience of elevated levels of consciousness here with you, and together you are creating a New Earth reality. You are stepping into new energy, into new levels of consciousness where so much more is available to you.

Allow, allow, allow. As you will remember, our dear friend, it is about opening and allowing. Open to the Source Energy that creates worlds, that flows through you. Open to the potential and the possibilities. Allow it to come to you. You are either doubting it, denying it, trying to figure it out, trying to make it happen, pushing, and forcing from an energy of lack, limitation, fear, and separation, or you are allowing the highest well-being that is always available to you in every moment.

This time on your planet is *the* most perfect time for you to fully step into being all that you are. It has been divinely orchestrated for you to come into the realization of the truth of who you are. This is the greatest thing going on *anywhere* in the universe. It is all about the experience of transformation of consciousness that is happening within you and all around you, and it's the best thing anywhere.

Embrace it, play, and have fun, and fully open to all that you are. It is going to be so beyond what you can even imagine as you let yourself into levels of consciousness that you have never experienced in physical form before. You are everything you wish to be. You already are. It is all within you and it always has been.

CHAPTER 3

TYPES OF CHANNELING AND ACTIVATING THE SENSES

Channeling is a natural, normal form of communication between humans and angels, guides, nature spirits, collectives, animals, pets, nonphysical beings, higher-self aspects, and the universe. Expressions of channeling are known, felt, and expressed in a wide variety of ways. The term channeling simply refers to the translation of consciousness, higher wisdom, and/or Source Energy into a physical experience. It is a means by which the non-physical communicates in our physical world. While not everyone deliberately receives higher wisdom and translates it into words, as a channel does, channeling is similar to things like hunches, intuitions, and a state of being in the flow that most of us experience from time to time in our lives.

In this chapter, we will discuss the many ways that channeling might already be expressing through you without your awareness of it. In fact, if you followed through with the automatic writing exercise in the previous chapter, you've already started! We will explore forms of channeling that you might be unfamiliar with. We will also review many common ways of channeling. The important thing to remember is that if you are drawn to channeling or channeled information, you are a channel, and the many expressions of channeling are available for you to explore.

All forms of channeling are a manifestation of the one consciousness comprised of Source Energy and infinite intelligence. Some people think channeling is limited to an experience when a specific entity uses a person's mind and speaks through them. While this is true for some people, this is not the only form or even the most common example of channeling. We will explore many expanded experiences of channeling in this book.

Whether you are channeling your higher self, soul, angels, archangels, guides, beloved pet, collectives, or your own council, it is all an expression of the one Source that is oneness consciousness. There is nothing alien or out there. It is all coming from the field of consciousness known as the One consciousness, oneness, or as The Council refers to it, All That Is.

Many books, movies, poems, songs, designs, technological advancements, and inventions were channeled from a higher consciousness and manifested into physical form in our Earthly world. In many of these cases, a person likely didn't know they were channeling or even have any familiarity with channeling. They would not identify it as an entity using their mind, but potentially explain it as accessing something deeper or inspired.

Other people do hear a particular voice, like Helen Schucman, who channeled and dictated the well-known book, *A Course in Miracles*. She explained that the entire book had been dictated to her, word for word, from Jesus. Helen was a clinical psychologist who heard a voice that said, "This is a Course in Miracles. Please take notes." This is how her experience of channeling began and *A Course in Miracles* was created.

Everyone opens up to higher wisdom in their own unique and personal way. There is no requirement, no one-size-fits-all, and no one way that works for everyone. Some are consciously aware that they are channeling, and many others are not. Some people find automatic writing to be easy and effortless. Others find it difficult and gravitate more toward their interest in verbal channeling or animal communication. Some have completely spontaneous experiences of receiving higher wisdom or communication from a loved one on the other side with no prior knowledge of being able to channel.

We've all seen examples of performances that seem to go beyond human capabilities. A first responder during a crisis, or a mother who lifts a car off her child are examples of this type of transcended experience. Still, there are many other instances of people opening up to a higher state of being that are easily overlooked because they are so common.

When an athlete, musician, artist, or speaker is "in the zone," this is a term that refers to channeling. This form of channeling is usually an example of Source Energy flowing through a person that translates into the physical form of an exceptional physical performance or beautiful creation. Channeled connections are often easy to recognize in creative expressions like writing, painting, dancing, and other artistic mediums, but they occur in every area of life. Such creativity is often referred to as inspired because it seems to come from another place.

At the heart of channeling is the ability to open up to something more than the limited human self. This happens in countless ways for us when we are present. However, with practice, it can happen more and become a way of living. Channeling is, truly, a very natural thing.

We are going to explore several examples of channeling that you may or may not be familiar with. They are automatic writing, verbal channeling, conscious verbal channeling, trance channeling, mediumship, Light Language, animal communications, nature spirit channeling, healing, tarot, or card reading, and psychic channeling.

TYPES OF CHANNELING

Automatic Writing
Automatic writing is an ability that allows a person to produce written words without consciously writing them, or writing that is produced involuntarily when the person's attention is seemingly

not directed to an expected result or topic. It is a process or product of writing created without using one's conscious mind. Automatic writing is when a person writes without consciously deciding which words to put down on paper. Most easily explained, the written words seem to come out of nowhere through your hand and onto paper.

Automatic writing could be compared to journaling or could be present in the writing of a song, poem, screenplay, or book. It is believed that almost all great books and screenplays had an element of automatic writing where the content written seemingly came from some place other than the person's conscious or subconscious mind. For the purposes of this book, I describe automatic writing as a process to access guidance and advice from higher wisdom, spirit, your higher self, guides, angels, loved ones on the other side, or the universe.

Verbal Channeling

Verbal channeling is when a person vocally speaks out loud the channeled wisdom they are receiving. Verbal channeling is very similar to the experience of being a language translator or interpreter. When one is verbally channeling, you allow yourself to sense or feel the nonverbal communication, energy, vibration, and consciousness from higher wisdom, angelic beings, spirit, or nonphysical beings, and then translate it into human words and language that can be understood.

It's common for someone to close their eyes while verbally channeling, but not all verbal channels do so with their eyes closed. It is also common for a verbal channel to remember what they channeled or what information came through during the channeled experience. This is different from trance channeling, when the person has no awareness or memory during the channel.

Trance Channeling

Trance channeling is essentially where a person allows spirit, angels, higher self, collectives, or nonphysical beings to use their body as a vehicle to communicate with the human world. A trance channel often describes how their own consciousness completely moves aside or leaves the body entirely and another consciousness speaks through them. A common difference between a conscious verbal channel and a trance channel is that the trance channel has no awareness or memory of what was said during the channel.

Mediumship

Mediumship is when a person specifically channels a loved one or specific person now on the other side either for themself or as a medium for another person to communicate with someone on the other side. While a medium might also channel higher wisdom or angels, they have a unique gift of being able to communicate directly with a specific person now in spirit form. An example would be channeling a message from your deceased relative or being a medium for a wife who desires to receive a message from her deceased husband. We'll go more in depth on this art form in Chapter 17.

Light Language

Light Language is a cosmic language known and understood by the soul, but uncommon to any language on earth. It is accompanied by sound and energy to convey messages. Speaking or singing Light Language is when you use your voice to create frequencies matching the channeled vibration that you are receiving. It's common for someone to also move their hands to match the vibration and interpret the energy they are receiving. Speaking in tongues and chanting might also be considered forms of Light Language. It is a form of communication beyond the limits of the human mind. We'll explore Light Language more in Chapter 15.

Animal Communication

Animal communication is when someone transmits or translates a message from an animal, living pet, deceased pet, bird, dolphin, whale, or some other form of animal species. Communication between human and animal can often result in understanding an animal's desires, perspective, or feelings and can also cause some kind of change or improvement in the animal's situation or behavior when understood. Most commonly, an animal communicator will listen to what the animal has to say, then pass

YOU ARE A CHANNEL

the information on to the animal's human companion. An animal communicator can also share messages from a deceased pet to comfort a grieving human companion.

An animal communicator might also speak to or receive messages from a collective of animals within the species like the dolphin or whale collective. Animals can also communicate and express themselves through feelings and visualizations, which the animal communicator can pick up on and interpret. An animal communicator might also communicate back to the animal with feelings or visuals instead of words. We'll learn more in Chapter 16.

Nature Spirit Channeling

Nature spirit communication is when someone receives messages from the elements of nature like trees, flowers, plants, mountains, earth, oceans, etc. Nature spirit communication might also include elementals, fairies, and beings within the nature kingdom. Elemental may be described or experienced as gnomes, undines, sylphs, and salamanders. Nature spirit channeling might also include a component of the elements of nature: earth, water, air, and fire.

Healing

There are many healing modalities. Channeled healing is when the healer is channeling energy, vibration, and higher wisdom to the physical, mental, emotional, or spiritual body of the human. There are many types of healing such as Reiki, therapeutic touch, remote healing, quantum healing, and many other forms. Healing is often done while the healer and person receiving the healing are in the same physical location, but can also be done remotely or through the quantum field. This could include healing of people, animals, nature, land, water, or the earth.

Tarot or Card Reading

A tarot or card reading is when someone uses tarot cards, playing cards, or oracle cards to gain access to higher wisdom and spirit. People often use tarot or oracle cards to ask and answer specific questions or receive direct guidance about a subject. A tarot reader can use cards to channel messages for themselves or to receive channeled messages from spirits and angels for others.

Psychic Channeling

Psychic channeling is a form of gaining insight into one's past, present, or future. A psychic is generally reading the energy field and patterns of other humans and is tuning in to this realm versus higher realms. A psychic channel may or may not use tarot or oracle cards. It is common to use palms, crystals, stones, and like often seen in movies, a crystal ball of sorts. Psychics might be able to predict one's future or might be perceiving the potential or possibility of an event based on current energies and trajectory.

ACTIVATING ALL YOUR CHANNELING SENSES

There are many different ways to experience channeling. You can use all five of your physical senses to activate your channeled connection and help you go deeper into your experience. Your physical senses include what you see, hear, taste, touch, and smell. It's common for people to experience channeling through their sense of hearing or seeing. Most people likely don't think about using their sense of smell, touch, and taste, but they can be powerful senses to initiate or enhance your channeling experience.

Spirit can use any one of your senses to bring messages through to you or expand your awareness. In fact, spirit often communicates with us, or makes their presence known, through our senses. Once you are aware of this, you can intentionally begin to notice and interact with spirit through your physical senses.

I was teaching a class on channeling when I had one of the most joyful experiences of this. I was taking the group through a visualization to open their senses more deeply. The morning of the class, a friend had brought me a bouquet of freshly cut roses that I had put in my office.

When we focused the exercise on tuning in to our ability to smell, I immediately smelled the wonderful fragrance of the roses. Suddenly, I felt the presence of a beautiful energy in the room. My

YOU ARE A CHANNEL

eyes were closed, but I could see a pink light. As soon as I became aware of the presence of energy, I had a knowing that it was Archangel Ariel. I had heard of Archangel Ariel but knew little about her.

It was clear to me, through a sense of *knowing*, that it was her, even though I didn't *know* Ariel. Not having much familiarity with her, I later googled Archangel Ariel. Much to my surprise, the first article I found said that a woman who channeled Archangel Ariel always smelled the scent of roses and saw a pink light directly prior to receiving a channeled message from Archangel Ariel. These types of experiences are common once you open your channel to angels, guides, and ascended masters.

I had another experience one time while doing another group meditation. I smelled roses even though I did not have any roses in my house. I could smell the roses as distinctly as if they were there. I also noticed a uniqueness to the rose fragrance that I had never smelled before. The next day, a friend of mine sent me a bouquet of beautiful farm fresh roses. They had the same exact unique smell. We are so much more than just our bodies and our physical senses. Once you realize the infinite, timeless field of consciousness that is available to you at all times, magical and miraculous things begin to show up in your life.

Using your senses to channel spirit, and to open to manifestation, can be very powerful. On another occasion, I walked into my kitchen and could smell cigarette smoke. I don't smoke and no one else had been in my house all day. Cigarette smell is one of those smells that usually agitates me, but in this case, it didn't agitate me at all. The smell continued to show up day after day. I finally decided to ask if there was someone *there* who wanted to connect with me, and instantly felt the presence of a powerful masculine love.

Without ever meeting him, I knew it was my partner's deceased father. This was early on in our relationship, and he hadn't shared much with me about his father. However, I just *knew* it was him.

I asked his father if he had a message for me. Then, I sat down at my desk with my journal open. I felt the most incredible presence of love all around me. I used automatic writing to receive his message, which was about his love for his son, my partner. The entire time I kept seeing an image of my partner as a little boy with a huge smile on his face wearing a Little League baseball outfit.

Later that day, I asked my partner, "When your father was alive, did he smoke?" He replied, "Oh, yes, he did." I told him that I had been smelling cigarette smoke and had asked if there was someone in spirit who smoked that had a message for me. I told him that his father had come to me and I shared the message he had given me. It brought tears to his eyes as I read his father's words to him. We then shared a wonderful conversation about his father and his life. I could feel his father's presence the entire time.

The ironic thing was that my partner also shared that he had been smelling cigarette smoke lately as well. It was an amazing experience for both of us. Some months later, we were looking through a photo album from my partner's childhood, when there, on the page, was the *exact picture* of the image I had seen of my partner as a young boy. He was dressed in a Little League baseball outfit holding his favorite cat with a huge smile on his face and pure joy in his eyes.

You can also use your sense of taste to open your channel to spirit. Let's say for example that one of the things you remember most about your beloved, deceased grandmother is the wonderful banana bread she used to make. You can remember walking into your kitchen and smelling the banana bread baking. If you want to open to receive a message from your grandmother in spirit form, you can use this memory of smell to connect.

Close your eyes and take some deep breaths. Move your awareness from your head down into your heart. Now imagine you are back in your grandmother's kitchen. You might imagine her in her favorite dress and apron. Notice the colors of her dress, apron, and hair as they appear to you. What did the kitchen look like? Are there any sounds you remember?

Now remember what the banana bread smelled like—oh, delicious. Keep focusing on the experience until you are there in the kitchen with your beloved grandmother again. Did she have a certain perfume that she wore, or colored lipstick? Focus on every detail until you feel as if she is right there with you in the kitchen.

When you feel her presence around you, ask, "Grandma, do you have a message for me?" Allow your own awareness to be in the area around your heart. Allow your conscious mind to relax and just feel into the energy and presence of your grandmother as her consciousness begins to move into your field of consciousness. Even as I write this, I can feel my own grandmother here with me. And her message is, "Oh, life is so good. Enjoy it to the fullest. Have fun. Enjoy your life, Honey."

You can use any of your physical senses at any time to connect with anyone. Call to mind the specific person you want to connect with or communicate with. Close your eyes, take some deep breaths, and go from your head into your heart. Think of a picture of them that you cherish most or a memory of a happy time together. Go into as much detail as possible using your sense of sight, smell, hearing, taste, and touch. Continue to focus on your loved one until you feel as if you are back in that experience. Feel as if they are here with you and all around you. Once you feel them, ask for a message, or ask for them to touch your cheek, hug you, or gently stroke your hair. In my experience, they are eager to present themselves to us through our senses.

These are just a few of the magical, miraculous types of experiences that are possible for you when you open your channel to higher wisdom. Your senses are a powerful tool for tuning in to the eternal, ever-present consciousness of anyone and everyone. Your focus and ability to feel your way into an experience with a loved one will quickly allow you to reconnect with them, communicate with them, and continue your beautiful, loving relationship with someone on the other side.

CHAPTER 4

THE CHANNELING RELATIONSHIP

Living a channeled life is why you're here. You are here to be a channel of love and light in the world. You are an extension of Source Energy. Channeling is the inherent connection to your soul and higher wisdom that exists to support and guide you through the human experience. Once you fully open to your channel and the power it possesses to change your life, everything in your life begins to transform, becomes easier, more fulfilling, and more expansive.

When one forms a relationship with one's soul through the process of channeling, it often becomes the most important relationship in one's life. It's like a best friend who is always there for you day or night. It's the one relationship that will be with you every moment of every day for your entire life. It loves you unconditionally, knows the highest truth of everything, knows who you really are, knows what you're capable of, believes in you more than anything, and will never hurt you, leave you, or judge you.

It's the most important relationship you'll ever have. If you hold it as such and treat it as such, you will have the most intimate, loving, transparent, communicative relationship with your channel that you could ever imagine. *It is your best friend.* It is the love of your life. It's your soulmate.

Make time for it, commit to it, devote yourself to it. It's a relationship, just like any other relationship in your life. If you make time for it, trust it, enjoy it, love it, the relationship expands and grows. Also, just like any relationship in your life, if you're constantly doubting it, if you're too busy, if you don't trust a word that it says, if you're contradicting it, you're not going to have a great relationship. Think about what makes a great relationship: communication, trust, love, devotion, and spending time together.

Cultivate your connection and relationship to your soul and the infinite intelligence that is always available to you in the same way you would your soulmate or the love of your life or your best friend. The result: You will have a relationship where you know you are never alone, they are always with you, they are this aspect of you that is in a higher dimension of consciousness, that has the grandest view of what's going on, always loves you, always celebrates you, always accepts you, always knows what's in your highest good. Why would you *not* want to have a relationship with that? Just like any other relationship, when you are devoted to it, committed to it, spend time with it, and trust it, you will cultivate a very expansive, beautiful relationship with your soul.

Imagine if you were in a relationship with someone and continuously felt that they are never there for you, they never show up for you, they don't make you a priority, you don't trust them. It's unlikely that would be a fulfilling relationship and doesn't represent the type of relationship most would like to have. Often, we unknowingly think and feel these things about our soul and Source. Many people experience this kind of unfulfilling relationship to higher wisdom because they do not know how to develop a connection with their soul.

Can you think of a person in your life who only calls you or spends time with you when they have an issue or problem? Have you ever had a friend who only calls when something's wrong, to complain, or wants you to save them from some drama? Or even worse, the person calls only to blame you for when something goes wrong in their life, or to tell you how it's all your fault because you weren't there for them? We often do not realize that the only time we devote our attention to our relationship with our soul, Source, or higher wisdom is when we have a crisis. For example, praying for help or answers when something has gone wrong.

Don't just tune in to higher wisdom when you have a problem or you're upset or you need money. This relationship can be everything you want it to be, and your physical human relationships will be a reflection of your relationship to your soul and Source. If you're looking for the love of your life, you are looking for your relationship to your soul. Once you cultivate that relationship within you, all other relationships will begin to reflect back to you the loving, unconditional, rich, fulfilling relationship that you have created with your soul and Source.

It's a lifestyle. Make time for it. Commit to it. Be devoted to it each day. Approach it like a relationship with your soulmate or your best friend. It's a deep, intimate relationship that's always growing and always expanding.

You might start to notice the energy and evidence of your relationship to your soul and Source in your everyday life. You can open this awareness more fully through your physical senses. An example might be smelling the beautiful fragrance of a rose. Then, imagine that you are inviting your soul, higher self, or Source to experience smelling the beautiful fragrance of the rose with you or *through you*. Soon you will realize that connection is always there and always available.

Early on in my channeling I was doing a private session with a woman who wanted to connect to her soul and angels. The Council told her when she was brushing her hair in the morning to invite in her soul and angels to have the experience of combing her hair with her. I was intrigued and decided to try it for myself. One morning I was combing my hair and thought to myself that I was going to invite in the presence of my soul and angels to comb my hair with me. All of a sudden, this energy came through my head, into my hands, and then into my entire body. It felt like a million angels were brushing my hair in that moment. I could feel as if each one of them were gently brushing through each individual hair on my head while in a state of pure bliss and delight. It was truly magical.

And that's just the beginning! Food tastes better. The flowers are more beautiful. Nature is more alive. The air is cleaner. The animals become more sacred, and you feel a sense of deep love for all beings. So many things will open up as you come into this connection. You, too, can begin to consciously and intentionally tune in to this relationship with your soul, higher self, angels, and Source. Things will show up for you on levels that you've never experienced before.

One of my students, a woman from San Diego, was invited to speak at a Channeling Summit shortly after she completed the channeling course. She was honored to receive the invitation, and she knew she was taking the virtual stage with some highly experienced channelers. This was the very first time she had channeled for a group, and it was also the first time she had channeled live in front of an audience—but she wasn't going to let the opportunity slip by.

She felt that this live, virtual experience was a great chance to step out of the "spiritual closet" once and for all. She was searching for the perfect way to introduce her family to channeling.

The day of the summit, she began to realize that not only would her uninformed family and friends be watching, but so would other channelers that had been channeling for years. Her biggest fear was that her guides would not be able to find a happy medium for all in attendance.

She could only imagine the confusion that her 85-year-old father would feel by a question coming from an experienced channeler trying to get new information that had never been heard before. The fear was beginning to take over as she was introduced, and she wondered if she'd even be able to relax enough to bring in her guides. After telling her story she decided it was time to bring her guides in for a channeled message and some questions from the audience.

She took her three deep breaths, and sure enough her guides were right there, just as they'd promised they would be. She could hear the questions and the answers, but she wasn't really conscious of any of it. This is when the total trust took over, and a feeling of peace was with her the remainder of the time. She channeled for over 40 minutes. Although she didn't have much recollection of what her guides had said, she just knew she felt good.

As soon as it was over, her phone started ringing. Not only did the inexperienced ones enjoy the information, but the extremely experienced ones did too. Once she listened back to the session, she was very impressed by how her guides were able to go slow enough for the new ones, but also by how they kept pace with the difficult questions from the established ones. The lesson she shares here is you must always have faith in your abilities and never doubt your angels, guides, and higher beings. When they say they'll show up for you, they always will.

Channeling is a relationship and it's a lifestyle. Your channel is already here and open to you or you wouldn't be reading this. If you are drawn to channeling in any way, *you yourself are also a channel.* Anyone who's drawn to channeling or channeled information is a channel themselves. There are millions of people on earth who have never heard of channeling and never will, but for some reason, *you are a channel.* You drew this information to you and discovered this book *for a reason.*

So, it's a lifestyle. Treat it like your very best friend or soulmate and be devoted to it; trust it. We're going to talk a lot more about trust! Don't worry, we'll go back to that one!

A VISUALIZATION PROCESS TO OPEN YOUR CHANNEL

Take some deep breaths to your own count as you make the magnificent journey from your head down into your heart, stepping down, stepping down, stepping down into your heart. Imagine a doorway appearing in front of you as you move down into your heart. Open the door and step into the beautiful, powerful space that is your heart and the intelligence that lies deep within your heart. As you step into this sacred space, you step into the light.

Imagine yourself stepping into the light, and as you do, you become illuminated in the light. The light flows through you, surrounds you, and expands from you in every direction. Step into the light. Step into the light and set yourself free. Feel the freedom of being in the light. Feel the power of stepping into the light. As you illuminate every cell of your body from the top of your head to the bottom of your feet and out to your fingertips, the light gets brighter, deeper, fuller, richer. It begins to expand from you in every direction, filling the entire room with light, as you feel flowing to you and through you in every direction even more of this intense and beautiful illumination into the light of all that you are.

Now intentionally, consciously focus the light that you are down into the Earth beneath you, through the bottoms of your feet, down into the Earth, down into the roots of the trees and the crust of the Earth, all the way down to the center of the Earth. As you reach the center of the Earth, a powerful illumination emanates from the center of the Earth, flowing up like a spiral of energy in every direction, up through the bottom of the ocean, illuminating the entire ocean, all of the oceans illuminated.

The bright, beautiful light flows up and glistens and dances on the waves as it now flows over into the sand. And now imagine the light moves up through the water, over the sand, over the land, into the grass, into the trees. The light comes from you, the conduit of light that you are, into the center of the Earth, illuminating the center of the Earth and then floating up, shining through the oceans, up onto the shores, over the land. The light flows now into the rivers, and up the trees, through the grass, encompassing all of this beautiful, magnificent planet with light.

The light now floats up into the air, illuminating every particle within the air, the birds, the bees, the animals all illuminated in the light. And now, as you focus this conduit of light that you are from the bottom of your feet, down into the Earth, into the center of the Earth, up like a spiral of energy through the bottoms of the oceans, over the shores, onto the land, through the rivers, up the trees, imagine now the divine light flowing into the ground beneath every human right now. Feel it come up from the ground into the bottom of the feet of all of humanity, up, up, up until this light reaches the hearts of all of humankind, no exception.

See now all human hearts illuminated in divine light, see the light flowing up through the bottoms of their feet into their hearts, now flowing up to the top of their heads and out their fingertips until all of humankind has been fully illuminated in the light, from your feet into the Earth, from the Earth into the feet, into the heart, into the entire being. Now seeing all of humanity fully illuminated in the light and you, dear master, are the conduit of this divine light.

See it going from your heart into the heart of all of humankind, sending divine love, sending divine light, with no agenda, not trying to do anything, but clearly, confidently, powerfully focusing the divine light that you are, the conduit that you are of divine light, focusing your heart on divine love, sending divine love from your heart to all of humankind, sending your light, the divine light, into the Earth, into all of nature, into the hearts of the animals and into the hearts of your beloved human family.

See the entire planet surrounded with light, a light so bright, so powerful, so visible to all that in this moment all of humankind stops whatever they were doing and opens their hearts and opens their eyes and opens their minds as they gaze into the beautiful, divine light shining so brightly, looking around for the origin of this light until they look down and see that the light is coming up into their hearts, that the light is coming from their hearts, that this divine light is coming from within them, is shining from within them, and that everyone else is also illuminated in this divine light.

See all of humankind awakening in this moment to the divine light within you all, seeing the truth and the power of divine love as you feel even more deeply into this moment, illuminating your own being, shining even brighter. And each time you do, the light gets brighter within all of humankind.

See humanity awakening now, remembering. See them remembering the divine light within them. See your entire human family all in the same moment stopping whatever they're doing in awe of the power and the beauty of divine light and divine love, forever changed, forever awakened, forever illuminated in the light. And so it is. And so it is. And so it is. All that remains now is peace, harmony, well-being, abundance, love, freedom, beauty. All that remains now is peace, harmony, freedom, love, well-being, abundance, and beauty. And so it is.

Take a deep breath. Now let it go. You are an alchemist of light. You are a master. You are a conduit of divine light and divine love. You matter. What you focus on matters. What you see, what you feel, what you think, what you believe, what you envision—it all matters. You're powerful. Remember.

CHAPTER 5

ASCENDED MASTERS, ANGELS, AND GUIDES

Imagine having the ascended masters, angels, and your guides on speed dial to call anytime you need answers, guidance, support, or love. The truth is, they are always there for you, always available to you, always guiding you. Everyone has this connection and can learn to connect with the angels, ascended masters, and their guides.

My first experience of communicating with an ascended master was Jesus, who came to me one day in meditation. As a child, I loved Jesus. I grew up in a loving Christian family in a small town. I attended Sunday school each week and sang about God and Jesus's love. I was taught to pray before meals, praise the Lord, and keep Jesus in my heart, as he was the *only one true way*.

As I got older, I began to question the things I was taught about the Bible, religion, God, and Jesus being the only way into Heaven. My questions were often met with the same reply, "Well, that's what the Bible says." Conflicted and overwhelmed by the contradiction, I lost interest in religion. I stopped using words like God, and especially any reference to Jesus. In fact, during a period in my life, if someone mentioned the word *Jesus*, I would immediately get triggered and move away from the conversation.

You can imagine my surprise when after a couple of decades of denouncing Jesus, he would appear to me in a meditation. I instantly and without a doubt knew it was Jesus. He presented himself to me the way the Bible had always shown him, which was comforting to me for our first meeting. I immediately felt love for him and felt his love for me. There was no judgment, no demands, no dogma, only his strong presence of unconditional love. He held my hand and we walked together. I don't remember any particular message, just his presence, love, and him holding my hand.

Shortly after, a dear friend contacted me to tell me that her dog was dying. She was emotional and upset as the dog's transition seemed imminent. I talked with her in a calm and comforting way in hopes I could offer her some peace. Then suddenly, Jesus presented himself to me. He showed me an image of himself reaching down to pick up the dog. I remember how lovingly he picked up the dog, and I knew the dog was immediately out of pain. The dog then turned into a precious little white lamb, and Jesus carried the lamb into Heaven. I told my friend what I was seeing as if I were explaining a dream. After Jesus carried the lamb into Heaven, I said, "They are in Heaven now." Then, Jesus was gone, and the vision instantly faded. My friend looked down at her dog, and it was gone. It had peacefully transitioned.

I had a similar experience with Archangel Gabriel, whom I was not aware of prior to him coming to me in a dreamlike experience one day. This beautiful, large, angelic being came to me. I knew he was some sort of angel. I asked him his name and he said, "Gabriel." Again, there was no message, just his powerful presence.

Although my experience was very real and the name Gabriel was not particularly familiar to me, I started to wonder if I had made it all up. I brushed it off and went on as normal until a day or two after. I was calling the customer service number of a business. I dialed the number, and almost immediately the customer service rep came on the phone and said, "Hi! This is Gabriel." That same day, I was in the grocery store, and as I walked by a woman, she said, "Oh, that's my friend Gabriel." The next day I went to a restaurant, and the waiter's name was Gabriel. Each time the name appeared, I would have energy flood my body and I would get chills.

I felt the presence of Archangel Gabriel for several months, and then the energy receded. It's normal for an archangel, ascended master, or guide to present themselves to you and then completely recede immediately or seemingly over time. It's normal for you to be aware of their presence with no specific message, while others do actually receive messages. For me, Jesus is always around me and I can evoke his presence just by focusing my thoughts upon him.

Ascended masters, archangels, and guides come into our lives at different times, for different reasons. Perhaps to teach, lead, or guide us during certain times in our lives. Sometimes you will know or be familiar with who is presenting to you, like my experience. Other times, you will receive a name, and only discover when searching the Internet that others have also received messages or experienced the presence of these beings. Some explain that their name is not important, which can also be a normal experience.

I have a student from Palm Springs, California, that was first introduced to the unusual name of a being called Metatron during a guided session. While guided into his Akashic records, the student was told by Metatron that he, Metatron, is the *presence* that was and is the Akashic records. Then a month or so later, the student walked into a metaphysical store. Once in the store, he was immediately drawn to an interesting-looking pendant. He asked the store clerk if he could look at it. The clerk said, "Oh, Metatron's cube? Sure, here you go!"

Then a few months later he was awakened at 2:02 am and received his first direct message from Metatron where he clearly announced and introduced himself. He sat up in bed, grabbed a journal, and wrote the message that came. Metatron had appeared to him to lead and guide him through the ascension process. Metatron informed him that he would begin channeling and would be a wayshower into the New Earth. Although he doubted it at the time, some years later, that is now exactly what he is doing.

My students have many stories from all over the world about the introduction of an archangel, ascended master, guide, or divine being in their life. A wonderful man from California who participated in my course, The Art of Channeling, explained that one morning while in the shower, he kept hearing, "I am Commander Ashtar, I am Commander Ashtar." He jumped out of the shower, grabbed a journal, and started writing down the messages he was receiving, despite never hearing of a being named Commander Ashtar before. Later in the day, the student looked up the name on the Internet and found that Commander Ashtar had commonly visited those in the process of awakening.

While these connections are often spontaneous at first, you can initiate a connection with anyone and choose who you want to channel. If you have always felt or begin to feel a connection to a certain being, ascended master, angel, or saint, you can ask them for a message. Most always, that higher being will agree, and the connection is made.

At first, I didn't know this was possible, but one day I decided to explore whether I could ask a particular being to present to me and bring messages through me. I had always felt a connection to Saint Francis, so I asked Saint Francis to let me know he was there and give me a message.

Nothing happened. A couple of weeks went by, and still no message from Saint Francis. I found myself on a trip to Arizona, trying to use my GPS to get to a restaurant to meet a friend. I knew the general direction, but not exactly how to get there. All of a sudden, my GPS completely changed course and was now taking me in the opposite direction. I had no idea where I was going, but I knew it was not in the direction I wanted to go. The GPS took me down several *wrong roads* until I eventually ended up at a strange place that looked like a monastery. I heard as clear as day over my right shoulder, "Walk in."

It seems crazy to me now, but there I went walking into some strange place, no idea where I was, and certainly not where I had intended to be. Suddenly, I saw this magnificent statue. It was shockingly beautiful and quite tall. As I walked up to it, the name of the plaque beside the statue almost appeared to glow. It said, "Saint Francis." I was in tears, in awe, laughing, crying, and then sobbing as I kept repeating, "Thank you, thank you." It is as profound today as it was in that moment.

You are always guided, always loved, always known by the ascended masters, angels, and guides here to assist us on our path. You can call on them at any time for guidance and support. If you wonder whether you are really receiving a message from a particular guide or angel, trust yourself. They have come to you for a reason. Some will continue their presence in your life for many years to come, while others come and recede from time to time. They are loyal friends, companions, and teachers with unconditional love for you. Once you understand this, it's like having the ascended masters and archangels on speed dial, as one student has explained it.

A Message from The Council on Ascended Masters and Angels

We are so pleased to have the opportunity to speak with you all on this fine and glorious day indeed. We remind you that while our words are important, this is a vibrational experience. As you feel into the vibration that we bring forth, we invite you into dimensions of higher levels of consciousness where the truth— and the realization of all that you are—is always known and available to you.

In the realization of all that you are, know that all things— your soul team, your guides, your collectives—are always available to you and are an extension of you. There is no separation, not ever. They are always here with you, guiding you, offering you an awareness into higher realms of consciousness where everything is possible for you. They are not as separate from you as they may appear to be.

When you think of an ascended master or archangel, you are identifying with a part of you that has a power beyond what you are aware of in human form. It can be great fun for you to explore, develop, and play with integrating these parts of you and the power you have. For example, you might consider Archangel Michael as an archangel offering protection. You might evoke his power to protect you and your car before a long road trip. You will arrive safely at your destination, thanks to the powerful protection of Archangel Michael.

You are connecting into your power to elevate the vibration and the consciousness of your experience in such a way that you would be guided around any unwanted or potentially harmful experience. You could be driving down the road and something that is coming directly in your path will be unexplainably avoided. This is because of the vibration and the frequency that you have invoked into the force field of consciousness around yourself. It is your light and your energy that is protecting you.

You are a multidimensional being, with undiscovered power and abilities. The ascended masters, the archangels, the Pleiadians, the Arcturians, are all an extension of you reflecting and reminding you of the powers and abilities that you have as you focus your awareness upon them. You do have guides. You do have a soul team. There are many of you who identify with being part of a collective in that you are their ambassador here on Earth. And yes, all of that is true, but it is the only way your human can make sense of the God that you are, the pure Source Energy that is you, and your own oneness with All That Is. This is the highest truth of you.

Open up, play, and have fun with beings in higher realms, just like you would with your friends or your divine playmates here on Earth. What do you do as a child if you're wanting to play with a friend? You call them up and say, "Hey, do you want to play?" The archangels, ascended masters, your guides, and your soul team always answer yes to this question because they're always here, focused upon you, and ready to play and co-create with you.

You are in an experience of free will. While you might be saying, "I really want such and such to communicate with me," they are, we assure you. Open up and allow yourself to go beyond some of the limitations and limiting beliefs that you have about yourself. Our advice to you is simply to know that you are worthy of it, know that you are powerful, know that you are infinite intelligence expressing yourself in physical form.

Everything is *known*. When your human is trying to *figure it out* because your human is in lack, limitation, and pushing against what is, or when you say, "I have this terrible problem going on and I need to know the answer," you're holding yourself in a resistance and lower vibration that creates an experience of separation. You are in the 3rd Dimension of consciousness, where you are separate from the answers, separate from the solution, separate from your guides, separate from your higher self.

We will make this very easy. The most important thing that you can do to connect to your higher self, ascended masters, archangels, collectives, and your soul team and guides is to do the things that bring you joy and focus on what you love. When you're in the vibration of joy, that is the vibration most closely aligned to the truth of who you are. In this state of joy, you are more closely aligned to receive the vibration and consciousness of infinite intelligence, along with the guidance of your soul, guides, and higher beings.

You are everything you wish to be. You already are. It is all within you, and it always has been. We love you, we love you, we love you. And with that, we are complete.

COLLECTIVES, COUNCILS, AND STAR FAMILIES

Would you like to connect with your star family or the council of beings that helped you determine and design your life experience? Well, you can and it's easier than you might think. Channeling a collective or council of beings that are connected to your soul's evolution is quite common in the world of channeling.

Prior to channeling The Council during my QHHT sessions, I had no awareness of being able to channel anything other than a singular being like that which I was introduced to as a child. My only awareness of channeling back then was when a being from higher consciousness would come into a body while the consciousness of the person channeling receded from the body. The entity being channeled would then deliver their message. When complete, the channel would then come back into the body.

When I began channeling and doing automatic writing, I was surprised that the communication always referred to itself as "we" or "us." In time, I realized I was channeling a collective of beings who later identified themselves as The Council. They went on to say that it didn't matter what I called them and that any name I used would essentially be limiting the eternal, all-knowing Source Energy that they are.

They are a collective of ascended master beings who come forth to offer us a grander perspective on the human experience. Calling them The Council is the name that feels good to me, and it's the way I identify them to others. I have often had people ask if they are The Council of Light or The Council of Elders. These are collectives that have come forth to other channels who feel their own messages are very similar to that of The Council. The Council explains they are not separate from any of these collectives and simply encourage us to call them what feels most comfortable.

One of my fellow channelers explains that she has received many messages from The Council of Elders. She further explains that her understanding was that they are the collective of guides that help us to design our life experience, determine our destiny, and what we most want to experience in this life. The Council of Elders then watches over us throughout our life experience like guardian angels to ensure we experience and receive all that we have intended throughout our life.

Others might experience receiving channeled communication from a collective of star beings. The Pleiadeans, Arcturians, Andromedans, Lyrans, and Sirians are common councils or collectives of galactic beings that people might begin to receive communication from once becoming a channel. In my experience, I don't directly channel any of these beings. However, many of my students have shared that they had never heard of any of these collectives and then when channeling were given a message and told it was from the Pleiadeans, Arcturians, etc. Having never heard this word or name, many students then Google the name they were given only to discover it is a very common experience to channel information from them.

It is believed that these galactic collectives are highly evolved. Messages received from these collectives of beings are often to assist with the awakening and ascension of human consciousness.

They explain that they are distant relatives of humans who have already completed the ascension process and are most interested in supporting the inhabitants of Earth to do the same. They reside in a higher frequency and come through to guide us in the next steps of our evolution.

I've had several students from around the world that have shared a similar description of being contacted by their star families through automatic writing or verbal channeling. These star families may or may not be from one of the collectives of beings mentioned above. They all recount a similar explanation of being told they are an ambassador here on Earth for their star families. This is also a common experience and one that might explain why so many spiritually awakened people might describe feeling like they are *not from this planet.*

Just like your higher self, angels, and guides, you can open to receive messages from collectives, councils, and star beings. Simply by becoming aware that these beings are available to you might allow you to start perceiving the presence of their energy and consciousness. You can ask, "What does my star family want me to know?" As you begin to open to this connection more fully, you might also become curious as to exactly where your star family originated. I find that my students almost always receive an answer to this question either immediately or through a guided discovery process. If you are directed to a particular star family or collective of beings either through intuition or a message, trust it and allow yourself to be curious and open to the awareness that it presents to you.

PLAYFUL SCAVENGER HUNTS
AND SACRED TEMPLES

You might be wondering what is meant by a guided discovery process. I have found it to be one of the most fun parts of connecting to my angels and guides. A guided discovery process is when you are directed or led to information by higher wisdom either through dreams, clues, messages, or intuition. It's like a playful scavenger hunt designed and orchestrated by your guides for the purpose of showing you something important or attaining greater wisdom or knowledge about yourself, your world, and the higher realms.

One notable experience I had was with King Solomon, who came to me in a dream. In my dream, I was in a castle-like temple where King Solomon appeared to me with an important message. I felt like I had been in the castle before and was remembering it. Although I recalled the name King Solomon from the Bible, I had no idea who King Solomon was or the stories about him. From the moment I awoke from the dream, I became obsessed with everything I could find about King Solomon as if I were on some sort of search for a lost treasure. I watched documentaries, searched the Internet, and read passages about King Solomon from the Bible. I had no idea what I was searching to find or why I felt such a connection to King Solomon and the castle-like temple I had seen in my dream.

One day while searching for information, I came across a link on the Internet to the symbol of King Solomon. I didn't know that King Solomon had a symbol. When I opened the link, I nearly fainted. From the time I was approximately six years old, I have drawn a symbol repeatedly when doodling or drawing, never knowing what it meant. King Solomon's symbol was the exact symbol that I had drawn since childhood. Was this some sort of sign? Had I seen the symbol somewhere as a child and remembered something from my past? Was it a code to some higher knowledge? Or was it an experience I was remembering from a past life?

I continued with the scavenger hunt day after day, still feeling as if I were on a quest to find a lost treasure. The final piece of the puzzle was revealed when I came across the Temple of King Solomon in a painting. It was the exact same castle-like temple that I had seen in my dream when King Solomon came to me. I had chills in every cell of my body. I knew I had been there and knew it had some significance to me.

We might never know why we are guided to this information, but it is a common experience for people who are spiritually awakening or awakened, as well as people who are opening to channeling. It's important to stay open and not try to figure out why you are being guided to certain things, but to stay curious and have a sense of wonder. The clues often lead to some greater understanding in time, or assist in our awakening experience even without our knowing. For others, it leads them directly to their path and purpose.

One of my students explains a similar experience she had with the life and history of Jesus. She grew up in a strict Christian religious family where she was taught about the Bible and the story of Jesus's birth, death by crucifixion, and resurrection. Through a series of awakening experiences, she found herself on a spiritual path determined to answer her many questions about her purpose.

She was not pursuing any particular awareness about the life of Jesus at the time, other than what she had been taught through religion. She was out walking one day when she heard a voice say to her, "Jesus did not die on the cross." She was startled and shocked, as the thought seemingly came to her out of nowhere and was not something she had ever considered as a possibility.

Thus, her scavenger hunt began, and she started researching any information she could find on the life of Jesus. Much to her surprise, there were many books and documentaries that not only suggested, but offered potential facts and evidence that Jesus was married, had children, and never actually died on the cross. She found many other theories that were different from religious teachings, and even evidence that reincarnation had once been in the Bible, but later removed.

Although it was completely against what she had been taught, she knew she had been led to this information for a reason. She could feel the truth of it within her even if she could not explain how she knew it. Still determined to have a relationship with Jesus outside of Christianity, she began to channel messages directly from Jesus and later started sharing these messages publicly. While her views and research are not widely accepted by some in her family, she continues to share her channeled messages from Christ Consciousness, which are all about love.

CHAPTER 6

GIVING YOUR GUIDES AND ANGELS PERMISSION

My first experience of channeling was during a guided meditation and visualization session called QHHT, which stands for Quantum Healing Hypnosis Technique. My original intention for these sessions was not to start channeling, but to connect with my higher self and better understand my life's purpose. I had no idea that these sessions would open me up to channeling and meeting The Council. However, once The Council began to come through during this process, I couldn't get enough and did several QHHT sessions over many months. The QHHT practitioner would facilitate getting me into a relaxed, hypnotic state and then ask questions to The Council.

After many sessions, I started to explore channeling their messages on my own. I would lie down on a bed with my eyes closed and meditate. It would take me some time, but after about 15 minutes, I could feel the energy come in. I would turn on a voice recorder and allow their messages to come through verbally. While I would get messages, I still felt like something was blocking me from fully receiving what was trying to come through me.

During one of these self-guided meditation experiences, I said to The Council, "Use me, come on! I know I can do this. I am ready."

I immediately heard The Council say to me, "You're not fully giving us permission to come through. You've got to fully give permission." I became almost defensive and replied in my own head, "I am! What am I missing or not doing correctly?"

The answer didn't come immediately, but a few hours later, I realized that I was not giving them permission to fully come through. Truthfully, the last thing on Earth I wanted was for people to know that I was channeling a group of nonphysical beings, especially my family and most of my friends. While channeling The Council was the most loving, powerfully energetic experience I'd ever had, I feared what people would think of me.

As I dug even deeper into my feelings, I feared that I would lose my relationship with my dad, whom I loved so much. My dad is Christian and centers his faith around Jesus. Deep down, the little girl inside of me was afraid and felt she would lose her dad if she really allowed this to come through.

It was not just my dad, but my relationships with my family and many Christian friends. I was in fear of being judged or called crazy, even though I considered myself a very grounded, practical person. I didn't want to lose people that I loved. Yet I believed I might if I fully gave permission for the channel to come through and the messages made their way into the world.

One afternoon while I was listening to a recording of my channeling, I came to a moment of absolute truth and clarity. I came to a place within me where I felt, "I *can't not* do this. I've got to see where this takes me. I've got to see what this is all about and why me." I felt so strongly that The Council's messages were the greatest wisdom on the planet. Their profound wisdom had changed my life. It was the wisdom I couldn't find *anywhere,* and I had searched for years. I knew I had to walk through my biggest fear. It became clear to me that it was more important to share this wisdom with the world than the fears I had, even if that meant losing my relationship with the people I loved most.

I am happy to tell you that my greatest fears never materialized. While some of my family members do not understand or resonate with what I do, that's okay. I realized I had to be the one to accept and approve of myself. You are the only one who truly knows your own truth and how to live in a way that is authentic for you. I found the more I accepted myself and my channeling, others around me accepted it too.

Over the years, many people have shared with me the fears that came up for them. Some feel a genuine feeling they might be burned at the stake, ridiculed, ostracized, harmed, or killed for channeling their angels, guides, or heavenly wisdom. Others have shared they are afraid they are going to be isolated, embarrassed, or shamed. Most all expressed not wanting to be weird or woo-woo and are concerned what others around them might think of them. These are all normal feelings.

In my own experience, when I felt weird and woo-woo and felt uncomfortable about my channeling work, the people around me seemed to reflect that back to me. People pick up on your unease and discomfort. Without realizing it, I *was* the one putting out an energy of judgment about my own channeling and others simply reflected that back to me. When I realized it was coming from me, I had a huge shift. From that moment, I have never been concerned with what people think of my channeling work. I know that sharing The Council's wisdom with the world is what I am on this Earth to do.

Once I came into the feeling of absolute knowing that I was ready, I sat down and closed my eyes. I took some deep breaths and started to repeat over and over, "I fully give permission for my channel to come through." I noticed some fears would come up, but I kept repeating the words. After about five minutes, this energy flooded my body and tears began to stream down my face. I knew in that moment that my channel was fully open and everything was about to change.

I started sharing The Council's messages on social media and on my website. I created channeled courses, meditations, and eventually an online community. I later received offers to channel on podcasts, at speaking engagements, and to publish their wisdom in books. I love channeling The Council and sharing their profound and life-changing messages with the world. I can't imagine how different and dissatisfying my life would be if I had given into my fears and not fully given permission for The Council to come through me. As The Council promised so many years ago, I now live a life beyond my wildest dreams come true.

When you are ready for this profound and powerful break-through in your own life, come back to this chapter of the book and do the process that follows. If you are ready now, you can initiate the process of giving permission at any time. Begin by taking some deep conscious breaths and allow yourself to come fully into this moment.

GIVING PERMISSION

This sacred moment is between you and your heart, your soul, and your connection to Source. Take some deep breaths and go within to the truth of you. If it feels good, put your hand on your heart. Go within to the place in your heart, to the place in your being where you are safe, where you are whole and complete, where you are so loved. Everything is perfect in this moment. Become centered in this moment. Breathe yourself into a place of stillness and then create a sacred space within you and around you. Hold this sacred space for yourself in this moment.

As you feel into the sacred space in this moment, ask yourself, "Are you ready to fully give permission for your channel to come through? Are you really ready to fully give permission for your channel to come true? Are you really ready to give permission?" As you ask this question, just allow anything that comes up and anything that you feel, surround it with love, surround it with care and comfort.

Don't judge it. Just observe it and keep asking if you're really fully ready to open to Source, to open to higher wisdom, to open to divine intelligence. You may need to check in with that little girl or that little boy within you. You might need to reassure them that they are safe, that it's safe for them to do this.

Tune in to that little girl or that little boy and let her or him know that it is safe to fully open up and to play with your connection, and to rejoice in your connection, and to open fully and be who you are. You may need to bring into your awareness aspects of you and prior experiences of this life, or others. Reassure those parts of you that you are safe, that you are guided and protected and loved, that you are cared for.

It's okay to let go. It's okay to fully give permission for your channel to come through. Just check in with every part of you and bring every part of you into this moment. Shine the love and the light on every part of you. Reassure every part of you that you are safe, that you are loved, that you have been drawn into this moment at just the perfect time because it's time to fully allow. If you feel any resistance, just breathe into it with love and assure yourself that you can always come into the consciousness and the power of the moment, and that you are safe. Are you ready to fully give your channel permission to come through? Are you ready?

Invite in the most beautiful relationship with you and be who you really are. Allow the power within you and the love within you and the light within you. Are you fully ready? Continue to breathe in the love that is here for you. Continue to breathe in the light. If you feel any resistance, just breathe in the light. Surround yourself with light and love. Reassure every part of you that there is only love. There is only love. Now move your body into the feeling of openness and allowing, fully giving permission for your channel to come through. If it feels good to you, open your arms and allow, let go, fully allow, open up.

Just notice how your body feels, and notice the sensation you're feeling. Notice any emotion that comes up. It's perfect. Just take a couple more deep breaths and continue to give permission, continue to allow, continue to open, knowing this will always continue to expand and go deeper. In this moment, you're allowing. Now, take a couple of deep breaths. You can put your arms down if it feels good, or you can keep them there if it feels good. If you feel any sort of blocks, just continue to tune in to this energy. There is nothing blocking you. It's okay to take a little time with this process.

Whatever comes up, give it to the light. You may need to consciously, lovingly, tend to the little girl or little boy within you over the next few days or weeks, or any aspect of you that needs a little more time before it gives permission. For those of you who are here and now and ready, just continue to focus on being open and allowing. Take a deep breath and go even deeper into this moment. Imagine that there's a bright, beautiful light shining down upon you as bright and beautiful and powerful as the sun right there above you. As you take some deep breaths, breathe yourself into that light.

Take all the time you need to navigate any fears or feelings that arise for you. If something comes up, be gentle with yourself, be kind to yourself. It's okay. Don't judge your human or that little girl or boy within you. It's natural for your fears to come up when you consciously and intentionally focus your attention on fully giving permission for your channel to come through.

The process of fully allowing and giving permission may take some time. When you are ready, fully give permission to your channel, angels, and guides to come through. Your angels and guides will hear you and receive the message. There is no right or wrong way once you are fully ready to give permission for your channel to come through. Some people like to create a sacred place and ceremonial moment of fully giving permission. Others experience a knowing, and simply give their permission by saying in their head, "I'm ready and fully give permission."

You are a sovereign, divine being here in an experience of free will. Your permission to your angels and guides is an important part of the process of fully opening your channel. Allow all the time you need for this step of the process. It just might be the first time in your life that you actually give yourself permission to truly, authentically be all that you are. Then, be prepared for more love, freedom, joy, and fulfillment to come into your life!

One of my students, a man from Portugal, explains his experience, thus: "Channeling had been a big part of my life for many years when I came across Sara's work. I had been listening to and reading channeled information for many years. I often wondered how I could become a verbal channel, even though I had been channeling through music for many years.

"When The Art of Channeling course began, Sara asked us to make the commitment to being a channel. I did, and immediately, I could feel the shift. Straight away and without delay, the messages started to come. The energy felt really different in my body. I felt uplifted and nourished by an energy that was beyond anything I had ever felt before.

"My life has changed forever, and I love that I can now connect other people to their own guides, deceased loved ones, and Councils of Light, and see their lives change too. Sara is such a beautiful example of how living a life in alignment with higher wisdom brings such joy, fulfilment, and abundance. I am forever grateful to Sara for this magnificent gift within and always available to me."

CHAPTER 7

YOUR PERSONALITY, THE MIND, OR HIGHER WISDOM

A frequent question that arises when someone is learning how to channel is, "How does one know it's not one's own personality or mind providing the information that comes through when channeling?" Sometimes *it is* and that's okay. However, there is one fundamental and foolproof way to *know* you are receiving higher wisdom. Higher wisdom, your higher self, your angels have no judgment; they really don't. They will never offer judgment about you, your choices, others, or circumstances in the world. From the highest level of consciousness, there is only love and a much grander perspective of all things.

I've received questions while channeling about almost every conceivable topic that would warrant judgment or a stigma within the human experience. The Council has been asked about murder, genocide, suicide, abortion, abuse, addiction, war, politics, natural disasters, crime, theft, and many more sensitive topics. Never once have I ever felt the presence of judgment from them when answering questions on these subjects. They explain that what we call *terrible things* can only occur where there is a lack of consciousness present that leads one to the experience of separation, lack, limitation, fear, and desperation.

There is a knowing of the truth of who you are and an unwavering level of consciousness that will not go down with you into those lower levels of consciousness and start judging. If you notice any sort of judgment coming up in you while you are channeling, slow down. Take some deep, conscious breaths, slow down, and connect back into your heart. Don't push yourself or judge yourself. Just slow down, take some deep breaths, and come back into your heart. It's okay to pause or take a conscious moment before proceeding.

From a higher perspective there is no fear, there is no judgment, there is no worry. There is no hierarchy. There is no one better than another. There is an understanding that we have all been all things on a journey through levels of consciousness.

Higher wisdom exists in a vibration where there is no fear, no judgment, no lack and limitation, and no perspective of right or wrong like in our human experience. There is always a grander perspective. There is an innocence. Innocence is not being attached to what comes through or having an agenda.

Students have asked over the years why, if higher wisdom does not judge, have they heard other channels judging or condemning someone or a group of people while in channel. One particular channel a student asked about is a woman who I know personally. Much of the channeled information she brings through is loving, innocent, joyful, and expansive. However, sometimes when in channel, she condemns certain people and speaks of the wrongdoings within political parties and organizations.

A channel has the ability to override what is coming through from higher wisdom, and change the information based on their own beliefs. The expression of channeled information is a collaboration between the higher wisdom offered and the person interpreting or translating the message. You might notice that you resonate with some parts of a channel's messages and not other parts. You might notice that you feel an energy during a channel's message and then feel that energy change. That might happen when someone's beliefs are not fully allowing the message from higher wisdom that seemingly contradicts their own beliefs. Always trust yourself and take what resonates for you.

If you're starting to feel a lot of judgment or fear or any of those things coming up while you are receiving messages from higher wisdom, let go of your attachment. Let go of any need to change yourself, someone else, or the world around you. Come back into your innocence. Come back into a state of oneness. You will instantly know that *all is well*. When you feel that state of being that all is well, there is no judgment. And then things begin to flow, and you are back into alignment with pure love.

When you get into a channeled state, you feel *pure love* and often a feeling of oneness. You can also get yourself into a channeled state by focusing on the feeling of love and moving yourself into a state of pure love. The first time I was asked to channel for a group, I was unsure and hesitant because I didn't know if I could do it. I had only channeled for people one on one.

I arrived at the home where the group channeling was to occur. The host had placed a chair for me in front of rows of chairs where those in the group would sit. She asked everyone to sit down, and I took a seat in the chair in front of the group. I felt nervous for a moment, but almost immediately I felt love beginning to channel through me. I felt guided to say nothing but to look deeply into the eyes of each person in front of me. While saying nothing, I began to look into each one's eyes, and as I did, the feeling of love expanded and expanded. I felt love flowing through my heart and into every cell of my body. My body felt electrified, and I could feel my vibration rising higher and higher.

I suddenly noticed that I had absolutely no awareness of any features or characteristics about any of the people sitting in front of me. I had no judgment of whether they were old or young, thin or heavy, dark haired or light, attractive or average looking. There was only love. They were only love, pure love. As soon as I became aware that there was only love, The Council explained that this is how they see each and every one of us. That was the truth of each of us. And immediately, they came through and I began to channel.

CONNECT TO YOUR CHANNEL

Anyone can use this process to get into channel or to connect into a state of pure love when they are with others. Focus your eyes upon another until you no longer see their features. You might look into their eyes as if you are seeing them through your heart. Focus on feeling the love between your heart and theirs until you see and feel only love. This is the door that opens to higher wisdom.

You can practice this with a friend or family member, even when you're not attempting to channel. You can also use a picture of yourself or someone else and focus on seeing yourself or the other through your heart until you feel pure love and oneness without any judgment of features or characteristics.

Another common question from students is whether they are really channeling when they can hear their own thoughts or doubts when channeling. One particular student comes to mind who is an incredible verbal channel. During group channeling classes, when she was learning how to channel, she would offer to channel for the group. The message was always excellent and even included the answering of questions offered by other students. When the channeling ended, she would often explain that she could hear her own doubts of herself and what was coming through while at the same time channeling verbally.

I had this experience myself when I first started channeling. It can be a normal experience when verbally channeling, doing automatic writing, or any other form of channeling. It does not mean you are not channeling. In time and with practice, the voice of doubt in your own mind will fade. Keep going and trust yourself.

One of my students, a woman from Australia, explains, "I had been journaling and automatic writing for many years, but never thought of it as channeling. It always felt good and true but I didn't think anything of it. By working with Sara, I realized that all my channeled messages started the exact same way saying, 'Love. Love is all there is.' It was only looking back that I observed that the previous automatic writing had started the same way. I had never noticed as I didn't associate the writings with channeling.

Once I understood that it was common for channeled messages to start the same way each time, I realized I had my own starting phrase for my channels.

"I created a quiet comfortable space to allow myself to drop into my heart, breathe, and be open. Following Sara's guidance, I gave myself permission to *just be* without expectation. The channel came through *every* time without fail. Some days it was a shorter channeled message, and other times it was longer.

"No matter the topic, whether I was asking, 'What does my soul want me to know?' or asking a question on a particular issue, trigger, or person, there was absolutely NO judgment. The grandest perspective always came through, and consistent practice allowed me to trust and know I am not making this up. I was consistently told 'all is well' or 'all is perfect,' and by the end of the channel, in that moment, *it was*.

"The wisdom that came through brought forth an awareness or perspective that I had not considered. The clearer perspective allowed me to start from a more neutral position and be an observer rather than a victim. The feeling of pure love from which the words fall onto the page or were spoken verbally are something that can only be understood when experienced.

"I was aware of what I was writing, but sometimes wondered if it was making sense. It was only upon reading it back out loud once finished that I realized the magnificence. The choice of the words was succinct and beautiful. I was blown away by the magic of the experience. The humor that would sometimes come through was a great surprise. The hilarity and playfulness would be enough to shift my attention and focus to what is *really* going on. Laughing along while reading it back, seeing the words, hearing it spoken, and then feeling it, I knew it to be absolute truth.

"I knew this work was beneficial, but it is only now that I realized how big an impact it has had. The realizations and confidence in myself in many areas of my life is enormous. I am so excited to see what it will expand into on my journey in this lifetime."

Channeling is like any other ability, talent, skill, or art form. It takes practice. The more you practice, the easier and more fluid your channeling will be. You will be able to get into a channeled state more quickly and with less effort. You will likely be able to channel for longer periods of time the more you practice.

It is also important to note that you are not a dictation machine. Channeling is a relationship, and you are always encouraged to honor yourself and your truth. Channeling is not just one-way communication, like many people think of it. Your questions, feedback, information, experiences, and desires are equally as important to your angels, guides, and higher self.

In time, you will cultivate a beautiful connection between your mind, your heart, your soul, and higher wisdom. Your mind will begin to allow your connection to higher wisdom without so much doubt and second-guessing. You will begin to integrate every part of you to realize the power within you on every level. Your relationship with Source will be expansive, fulfilling, and fun! Enjoy the journey and the beautiful unfolding of becoming everything you are here to be.

CHAPTER 8

TRUST YOURSELF AND YOUR CHANNEL

This is quite possibly the most important thing that you will ever need to know about channeling: trust, trust, trust, trust, trust. I cannot emphasis enough that trust is the foundation of channeling. It will determine whether you continue with channeling or give up, whether you expand your channel and the wisdom you receive or feel stuck and disconnected, and whether you experience the love, support, and guidance that surrounds you in every moment or feel alone and isolated.

When you practice the art of channeling and tune in to higher wisdom, trust that you are not making it up, trust that you do have a connection to Source, and trust that it is always there for you. Trust, until there's no need for trust anymore and it becomes a *profound knowing.*

Early on in my channeling work, I was doing private sessions with people at their home. I had a client who had a session with The Council because she was having trouble with her husband and their teenage daughter. She had such an amazing breakthrough during her channeled session that she wanted her husband to have a session with The Council.

I can honestly tell you I have no idea how she convinced her husband to do a channeled session, but he agreed, and a few weeks later I did a session with him. During this time in my channeling work, I still questioned whether I was *making it all up*. I was conscious and aware while I was channeling and could even hear my own thoughts of doubt and mistrust while I was channeling.

This was certainly the case during my session with her husband. The session began. Her husband was nice, but I could tell he didn't really *believe any of this stuff* and seemed a bit standoffish with The Council. As the session progressed, the subject turned to his teenage daughter. He asked a quite serious question about his relationship with her. To which The Council was about to answer with, "Why don't you just dress up in a little pink tutu, dance around her bedroom, and have a tea party with her?"

I can remember it as clearly as if it was yesterday. In my head I said back to The Council, "Umm no! I'm not saying that. No way am I saying that! No, *we are not* saying that. He already doesn't believe this stuff. There is *no way* I'm telling him or letting *you* tell him to dress up in a little pink tutu and have a tea party and dance around."

All of this is going on in my head when suddenly I realized, *they had already said it.* In my experience, there was an approximately five-minute conversation in my head with The Council that they were not going to say that. When I listened back to the replay The Council didn't even pause; they said it and just kept going. By the time I realized it, I was mortified, and yet her husband seemed in peace and now very open to everything The Council had to say.

Shortly after, the session ended. When I opened my eyes, the husband had tears in his eyes. He said to me, "I will never doubt you again. Not even my *wife* knows that when our daughter was about 3 years old, I dressed up in a little pink tutu and had a tea party with her in her bedroom. *Nobody could have known that.* I get it! Thank you."

His wife later told me that his session had completely transformed his relationship with his daughter. They had a beautiful relationship after that. It was like a complete shift in perspective for him and it changed their lives. And it was a huge lesson for me in trust.

There have been many times over the years when I am channeling and The Council is about to say something that appears so strange, weird, or random to me. I remember one particular time on a live group call they wanted to say to the entire group (I am paraphrasing here), "The issue with your knee is related to this particular thing. You need to do this, you need to do that, and you can elevate your well-being into a place where that's no longer your experience. Your knee pain will be gone."

When I got off the group call, I was honestly embarrassed. It seemed like such a weird and random thing for them to say, especially to a large group. Within a few hours and in the days following, I received message after message from people who were on that call or listened to the recording who said, "That final message about my knee, that was for me. They were right! I did exactly what they said and now the knee pain's gone." It was another very important lesson for me to trust, no matter what I think of the message coming through.

You are not making it up. Trust yourself. Sometimes, the message might seem so random that you think you are making it up. It might even seem so easy or so *right there* that you feel like you're making it up. As you learn to trust, it gets easier and easier. In time, you will learn to trust it fully and you'll feel more confident. You will simply allow what wants to come through you without judgment of yourself or the information.

IMPECCABLE CHANNELING

It is also important to be impeccable with your channeling. You might receive information during your channeling that is for you and not to be shared with others. Several years ago, my sister was pregnant. She and her husband did not want to know the gender of the baby before it was born.

I was in my backyard one day when I spontaneously felt the energy of a child all around me. I could sense the child's personality and see a vision clearly in my mind. I knew it was my sister's child and I knew it was a girl. She was so playful, precocious, happy, and told me she would be coming soon.

As excited as I was about the visit from my soon-to-be-born niece, my sister did not want to know the gender of her baby before it was born. Even though I received the information, I knew it was not impeccable for me to say anything to anyone else in my family about my experience until after she was born. Knowing when and when not to share the messages you receive can also be an important part of channeling.

Someone asked me one time, "Why doesn't The Council tell us when something is going to happen or about current events before they happen or if someone is going to die or if someone has a disease before they are diagnosed?" Our angels and guides can only give us information that we can handle. It's determined by your ability to hold your connection and alignment based on your level of knowing. As we begin to perceive beyond judgment of circumstances and conditions like right or wrong, our guides and angels can share more information, if it's for the highest good. It is also determined by our ability to hold a higher perspective without going into fear. They cannot give us information that might harm us or cause fear.

I had an awareness one day that a dear friend of mine had cancer and was going to make his transition. I was also shown that this was the choice his soul had made, and it was time for him to move into a formless dimension of consciousness to continue his journey. I felt completely at peace without any fear or need to try to prevent his transition. I knew it was in the highest and best good and stayed clear about it. Not long after, my friend's wife told me he had been diagnosed with terminal cancer. She had not told anyone else and was devasted by the news. I felt I had been given that information and the vision in advance, so that in that moment, I could hold a peaceful, present, calm space for her to move through that experience with support and greater ease.

You have no idea how you are going to shine a light for others as you continue to open your channel. You have no idea the impact it will have and the ripple effect it will create. You might experience fear or doubt from time to time, *that's okay.* You have been given this amazing gift of channeling for a reason. Once you begin to trust and open to the wisdom that is available to you, the universe begins to use you in the most amazing ways as a conduit for the most beautiful miracles.

A Message from The Council on Trusting Your Connection

We are so pleased and delighted to have the opportunity to speak with you on this fine and glorious day indeed. We tell you that while our words to you are important, this is a vibrational experience of remembering who you really are, why you are here, and all that you intended when you chose this magnificent life experience. We assure you that life is meant to be so very good for you.

You are here for the expansion of your soul. You are here for the expansion of consciousness. You are here to express all that you are and to have the experiences you want to have for *you* as you explore and play and create as the master that you are having this magnificent human experience.

We could not be more excited for you and this time where you can live in a state of consciousness that you call Heaven on Earth or a New Earth. It is here for you now. It is available to all of you. There is something within you that knows and remembers that Heaven on Earth is possible for you. Allow it in.

You're in a human experience where many of you are in a dimension of consciousness where you experience separation. The 3rd Dimension is an experience of separation—good, bad, right, wrong. You think that you are your body and anything that is not your body, or you, is outside of you or separate from you.

Understand that as you reemerge back into the *Isness of All That Is,* which is possible for you as you elevate your own consciousness into a state of pure love, you come into oneness, you come into unity, you come into God consciousness, which means you are not separate from anything—ever.

Your vibration and the level of consciousness you are in determines which dimension that you are experiencing. Even though you are never separate from anything. We are not here and not there, and nor are you. There is a multidimensional nature where the consciousness that you are is not separated by geography or time or space.

You are us. We are you. You are The Council here on Earth. Just by being yourself, you are an ascended master being. You drew this conversation to you so that you could remember that.

You are a vessel and conduit of Source Energy. You are a conduit of light and love. You are Divine Love and *truth* in the world. You are a container of infinite intelligence, infinite love, infinite well-being, and infinite abundance.

You are living in exciting times. You are here for the greatest transformation of human consciousness that has ever occurred, and you are either seeing something like a war or a pandemic or a crisis, or you are seeing consciousness in action, love in action, transformation, transcendence, and revelation.

Do not lose your way. Do not get discouraged. Do not fight against yourself or anyone, because we assure you the battle never is out there. It is about consciousness in the moment and being present to a grander perspective, a higher awareness where anything and everything is possible for you and for all of humankind.

You can look around at current events and say, "Oh, that's terrible," no matter when you listen to this. You could always find something every day in your news, in your media to say, "Oh, that's awful, and that's terrible, and that shouldn't be happening. No, really this shouldn't. No, no, really, this really is bad. No, really this is awful. This really shouldn't be happening." You can justify and fight for your limitation and entangle and judge. And there is no judgment from our side ever, but you are either holding yourself in limitation and separation, or you are embodying the master that you are, the wayshower that you are in this moment, and creating new pathways, new levels, new frontiers. You cannot do that if you're entangled or feeling victimized.

There will always be something that, if you want to look outside of you for why you cannot find happiness within you, there will always be something you could use—what's going on in the world or in your family—as to why you cannot experience joy in this moment. And there is no judgment from our side ever, but that's how powerful you are. You are either perceiving Heaven on Earth or hell. They're not out there in the afterlife. They're states of consciousness here and now. They are a way of perceiving reality. They are a state of consciousness determined by your vibration and your frequency.

The only thing that changes anything is energy. The only thing that changes the body, the only thing that allows for spontaneous healings, the only thing that creates transformation in the body and your relationships with your families, with your children, is the energy that flows forth into new forms of manifestation, and this energy can only change through consciousness.

The greatest transformational force on your planet is love. The most powerful force is love. It could also be explained as consciousness, because as you elevate your consciousness and your awareness, there is only love.

Consciousness and awareness and love are what create change and transformation, but you do not have to entangle with lack and limitation and separation to experience the expansion that occurs through the elevation of your consciousness and your awareness, because consciousness is what summons the energy for grand, glorious manifestations in physical form. Consciousness, the elevation of consciousness and awareness is what moves the energy needed into form to create change.

When you really understand this, you no longer react to the external world. You will never again experience fear. You will not worry about anything. You will not struggle, and you will not suffer. And if you want to positively contribute to humanity and create a path forward out of suffering, the answer is consciousness, the consciousness that results in an unwavering force of love. And it is that force of love that can do the impossible because of the level of consciousness that summons the energy for great change.

Consciousness is what moves energy into form. It's the formula for all of creation. You have this awareness. Now watch it create miracles in your life and in the lives of others.

You can forget who you are. You can choose thoughts, behaviors. You can lower your vibration and your frequency. You can create stories and beliefs, and you can focus upon them until you completely forget who you are. You can blame it on everyone else because this is who they told you you were or who you weren't, and this is all the struggle and the things you went through, and this is why you can't be who you want to be. You can fight for your limitations, or in this moment you can perceive yourself into a level of consciousness and awareness where the truth is always available to you.

And in that truth, you remember you are free, and you always have been. You are divine, and you always will be. And it was never about anything out there. It was all within you. It always has been. It always will be.

CHAPTER 9

YOUR WAY
IS UNIQUE
AND PERFECT

There will never be and never have been two people who channel the *exact* same way. And that's a wonderful thing! Everyone's way of channeling is unique. Each person has their own special gifts, abilities, and expression of higher wisdom and Source Energy to share with the world.

I have taught over 5,000 people around the world how to channel, and there are no two people that are identical in their information, style, expression, delivery, or method. While many people have similar experiences when channeling or ways of channeling, it's as diverse as how an artist paints, a musician plays or sings, or an athlete plays. It's an expression that can only come through *you* the way it comes *through you.*

When I first started channeling, someone suggested to me that I go see a well-known channeler who had been channeling for over 30 years and was going to be doing a workshop in our area. I arrived at the workshop and awaited the channel's presentation to begin. She came on the stage, greeted the audience, and said she was going *to go get* the group of beings she channeled. Before she did, she explained that she had no awareness of what is happening once in channel. She closed her eyes and began taking long, deep breaths. Much to my surprise, she rather quickly opened her eyes again and began walking around the stage, engaging with the audience, and appearing completely *normal.* If it wasn't for her use of the term *we*, there was little difference in her appearance or speech. One would likely not suspect the woman was channeling.

I also noticed that the information was similar to what The Council was bringing through in their messages at the time. Her channel spoke of creating your reality, how to manifest the life you want, and how to elevate your vibration. The channeling went on for several hours and included questions with the audience.

While I enjoyed the workshop and information, I left feeling deflated and ready to throw in the towel. I did not channel at all like the woman on the stage. I assumed I must be doing something wrong in my own channeling because my way of channeling was different. My eyes were closed when I channeled, I often sat in a particular position with my fingertips touching, but I didn't walk around. I could remember what was being said by The Council when I was channeling. I knew where I was and what was going on around me. I did not have the experience of my consciousness leaving my body like this woman explained.

I also thought that because the information was similar and she was so much better known as a channel than I was at the time, that my channeled messages were not needed. I honestly thought about giving it up and no longer channeling. For several days, I didn't channel and felt lost and disappointed after seeing the woman channeling on the stage with her eyes open.

One morning, I awoke and felt the presence of The Council. I quickly grabbed my journal and began writing. They explained that they guided me to that workshop for an important reason. They said they were *here* and coming through me to now expand upon the information that was being shared during that workshop. They mentioned specifically that their message was the *next evolution* of the law of attraction into the concept of *true creation.* I suddenly saw a vision of the woman on the stage passing a baton to me like two teammates passing a baton during a race. I could see how she had brought a vast group of people to this level of awareness and understanding and now I was going to pick up the baton and run the next leg of the race. The energy of the vision was so powerful. It instantly refueled my passion for channeling and offered me a new perspective on what seemed to be some pre-determined destiny between The Council and me.

I immediately went back to channeling and felt even more excitement about sharing The Council's wisdom with the world. Some years later, I met several other channels during a live channeling event in Los Angeles. They were all around my same age and started channeling around the same timeframe. Every single one of them verbally channeled almost exactly like me. They would close their eyes, take a few breaths, and channel while seated with their eyes closed and often in the same unique way I would touch my fingertips. They also explained that they were aware and conscious during the channel, just like me.

The Council later explained that over the last several decades our consciousness and vibration has elevated to a place where it's no longer necessary for our consciousness to fully recede for the channel to come through like was common in the 1950s, 60s, 70s, and 80s. The woman I saw in the workshop had begun channeling in the 1980s when the consciousness and vibration were different. I also recalled other channels like Edgar Cayce, JZ Knight who channels Ramtha, and Jane Roberts who channeled Seth, who also started channeling several decades ago, explaining how their consciousness completely left their bodies while channeling. It all makes sense to me now and I realize the way I channeled was perfect and unique to me. Just like it will be for you.

Don't compare yourself to anyone or how they channel. Whatever way you channel and however your channeling expresses through you is perfect, and it will always be expanding and evolving. As you practice, your channel will likely become clearer and easier to access. Over time, you might go from automatic writing to verbal channeling. It's common to begin to access gifts, abilities, and skills you never knew you had.

One of my students, a lovely woman from the United Kingdom, who is an amazing verbal channel, comes to mind. Her channeling has expanded into so many new things since she began channeling. Her first experience with channeling was through animals. She spontaneously received a message from a lion and then the lion consciousness. While the messages were powerful for her, she later began to doubt her connection. In time and with some guidance, she discovered she could verbally channel and began to channel messages from animals, angels, fairies, and much more. Then, without any formal training as an artist, she began painting beautiful, detailed channeled artwork of animals who *came to her* with messages and wanted to be painted.

She explains, "Realizing that I am a channel has raised my consciousness, frequency, and vibration. Sara and The Council were divinely placed onto my path at a time when I thought I had lost my ability to channel the lion consciousness. Very quickly, Sara and The Council expertly guided me back into my connection with them.

"My channeling then took me on a journey of channeling many more animals, as well as angels, fairies, and ascended masters that have raised my consciousness, frequency, and vibration even more. Although I had no religious upbringing, I now channel Jesus and perform hands-on energy activations. I have realized my greatest dream: to walk in the footsteps of Jesus. I AM forever changed."

We will cover multiple different ways of channeling in this book. Channeling is the process of opening to higher wisdom and allowing the flow of Source Energy into your body and physical experience. Verbal channeling and automatic writing are two forms of channeling, but there are many more. You can channel through art, music, dance, writing books, songs, or poems, conversation, nature, sports, and movement. Others might naturally possess or discover their ability to channel animals or loved ones who have crossed over. I also find that many people are beginning to channel Light Language. Light Language has been compared to speaking in tongues where a person verbally speaks or sings tones and sounds that seem to be understandable to one's soul or spirit, but is not a language we are familiar with here on Earth.

Another student, a woman from the wild coast of Cornwall, UK, explains, "The way I have channeled, for as long as I can remember, is through song and a language that my brain doesn't understand completely, yet it feels so good and true. I have come to know this as 'Language of the Stars.' My partner and I have sung and played music together for years. After both taking Sara's course, The Art of Channeling, we were inspired to try something new and mix what we traditionally brought through with verbal channeling woven in. In that newness was also a sense of knowing it's always been. This is now the most natural normal thing for us to do.

"I am so very grateful for the doorway that opened into infinite possibilities with channeling.

"When something goes beyond the trusting and into the knowing, it is so natural. The most normal thing is the most extraordinary thing. It's all here, and yet we're always finding new ways as we remember who we are and what we've always been.

"Sara is an incredibly loving, present teacher. My life has blossomed and expanded in untold ways since coming into her sphere. I am beyond grateful."

Allow your channeling to take any form that is natural and authentic to you. While it might be out of your comfort zone, play and explore the ways of channeling that present to you. Don't compare yourself to anyone else. We each have our own unique ability to channel. Not everyone will or wants to verbally channel. Not everyone who channels communicates with animals or deceased loved ones. Have fun with it, and allow it to lead and guide you to undiscovered gifts and abilities that lie within you!

A Message from The Council on Your Infinite Worthiness

We are so pleased and delighted to have the opportunity to speak with you all on this fine and glorious day indeed. We remind you that while our words to you are important, this is a vibrational experience that is allowing you into the truth of all that you are, so that you can remember who you really are, and why you are here, and all that you intended when you chose this magnificent life experience. This is the vibration of embodying and knowing your purpose for being here.

Your infinite worth is the promise of your life experience that nothing that has ever happened or could ever happen in this human experience that you are having could ever threaten or diminish your infinite worthiness. There's nothing you have ever done or has been done to you that could ever threaten or diminish how worthy you are as a soul, as a human, as Source, as the Divine. Absolutely nothing.

When you really come into the knowing of your value, and how valuable you are, and you allow yourself into the state of knowing your infinite worthiness, we assure you the desires of your soul will manifest in the highest form to surprise you, delight you, excite you, and amaze you.

Many of you have never consciously intentionally realized how worthy you are of everything you have in your life. The sun in the sky stays in perfect proximity to the Earth for you so that you can experience life on Earth, so that you can come into this experience and have everything you need and more. Every resource on this planet is here *for you*. The Great Creator, Source, God, the Divine knows your worthiness, never doubts your worthiness, knows nothing could ever threaten your worthiness, and allows you to focus yourself from oneness with the Source of All That Is.

Because you are so worthy, the Divine encourages you to focus yourself into your own unique expression of consciousness. You are so incredibly worthy, you are encouraged to incarnate into physical form on Planet Earth for the absolute purpose of your joy, your delight, your expansion, your expression of all that you are, for you to choose any and every experience and adventure you want to have for you.

It's as if Source said to you, "Think of the most elaborate, unbelievable, once-in-a-lifetime vacation that you want to go on. Where would you like to go, how long would you like to be there, and where would you like to stay? The finest hotel, or a quiet, intimate peaceful bungalow? Do you want to go on a cruise ship? Do you want to rent a beautiful home or have a beautiful home while you're on your grand adventure? It's a once-in-a-lifetime vacation, once-in-a-lifetime trip to anywhere you want to go. What do you want to do while you're there? What do you want to see? What experiences do you want to have?"

There's no limit. There's no budget for this trip. Source might say to you, "Anywhere you want to go. Anyplace you want to stay: oceanfront suite with the greatest view, mountaintop suite with an endless view of the mountains and the waterfalls and the valleys." Whatever it is for you. Source said to you, "The vacation of a lifetime. What do you choose?" That is how worthy you are. That is how valued you are.

You packed your bag, you focused your consciousness, and you incarnated into this incredible Earth experience knowing how worthy you are, how loved you are here on this grand adventure of your choosing. Everything is here for your experience.

You have always been the *most worthy*. It has nothing to do with any physical possession or anything in form whatsoever. There was a vibration and a frequency within the knowing of one's own worthiness that drew to them the resources for their experience to be what they desired. There is no hierarchy here.

You are worthy of the highest joys of life, and you have experienced them. No matter where you are right now on your grand adventure, you have experienced some level of joy, some level of well-being. You've experienced some miracles, some magical things, some level of abundance, some love. You are worthy of the highest experience you've ever had, and you're worthy of experiencing it in *every moment of every day*.

If we were to give you an example of living at the highest level of worthiness, you would come to realize that in knowing your worthiness, all that would remain in your experience is an unwavering, unconditional state of pure love, Heaven on Earth.

Many of you have spoken of Heaven on Earth, a New Earth, the 5th Dimension, this place we call pure love. If you were to start where you are, it would be to start in a state of pure love, because that is *what* you are, *where* you are. If for any reason you're not there, it's because you're denying your worthiness due to some circumstances or conditions that you are perceiving as limitation. That's all it is.

The eventual manifestation you will experience, through this understanding of your inherent worth, is unconditional love for yourself. To know yourself beyond uncertainty and doubt, to know yourself beyond pain and hurt, to know yourself beyond the wounds you've experienced, to know yourself beyond the guilt and the shame, to know yourself as you have never known yourself in this life.

On the other side, when you reach the top, when you get to the summit, what will you see? Endless beauty, endless abundance, endless well-being, endless freedom, endless joy, endless peace, endless harmony, endless expansion, endless inspiration, endless unconditional, unwavering pure love.

We are always with you. We are always available to you. You are everything you wish to be. You already are. It is all within you and it always has been. We love you, we love you, we love you. And with that, we are complete.

GET YOURSELF A BUDDY

I encourage anyone who wants to practice verbal channeling, mediumship, animal communication, Light Language, or any other form of channeling, to find a *buddy*. Find someone you trust and feel comfortable with and practice channeling with them. This is also a great way to share your automatic writing and take turns reading your channeled messages to each other.

A buddy can be anyone that you trust and feel comfortable with. Many people chose a close friend or family member. Your buddy might also be sharing channeled information or messages. Some buddies might also be sharing channeled messages, while others might simply provide a safe, comfortable place for you to practice.

Others might feel they have no one in their lives that could be a buddy for them. This is understandable. There are several ways for you to find a buddy. You are likely familiar with the saying, "When the student is ready, the teacher appears." I have found the same to be true with channeling. Make a clear intention that you are looking for a buddy to practice channeling with and then allow that person to come into your life. It might also be someone you know, that once you give permission for your channel to come through and set your intention to find a buddy, suddenly shares with you that they are reading channeled material or are open to things like this.

Within our community, there are approximately 5,000 people from around the world who have gone through The Art of Channeling series of courses. There are also many other platforms online specially focused on other channeling modalities like Light Language or animal communication. You might even be connected to many of these people because of your interest in things like spirituality, consciousness, and channeling. Once you set a clear intention and begin to focus on a buddy, the connection will be made. Who wouldn't want the opportunity to ask questions of their angels, spirit guides, or Source through you, the channel of higher wisdom?

On the other hand, I was not even aware of the importance of finding a buddy to practice channeling when I met mine—the woman you met in the Introduction, who helped me, through hypnosis, to connect with The Council. As you know, this seemingly spontaneous meeting changed the course of my life forever.

Without my buddy, I might not have ever discovered my ability to channel. I certainly would not have stuck with the process or learned to trust what was coming through me without her support and eagerness to ask them questions. Although I wasn't intentionally making the request to channel or find a buddy, something much greater and wiser was guiding us to meet one another.

Once you find your buddy, it will likely be obvious to you whether they are holding space for you to practice channeling or whether you are both going to take a turn asking questions while the other opens to allow higher wisdom. In my case, it was always my buddy asking questions and me channeling the answers. However, for many people, their buddy is also a channel so you might take turns.

Having someone ask you questions while in a channeled state is very important. Oftentimes, when I tune in to The Council myself, I reach a state of consciousness where I feel pure bliss and I have a sense of *All That Is* and all that is known. From that state of awareness, I have no questions.

Either you or your buddy can generate the questions. They might be personal questions or questions that are broader. There are no wrong questions and you don't need to review your buddy's questions prior to channeling.

You might also notice that highly specific questions don't always get specific answers. My buddy would often ask questions about an exact timeframe of when something would happen. The Council would always bring in amazing answers and information that expanded our awareness, but they often would not give an exact timeframe of when things would occur. They would often explain that this was because of the free will of all involved in the unfolding of circumstances and events.

One of my students, a woman from Florida, shares her experience with finding a buddy. "My channeling journey unfolded in a perfect way. I had been following Mike Dooley during the isolation of Covid and had been keeping a journal every day for years before that. When he introduced Sara and The Council, it was choiceless to join her The Art of Channeling course. As I now know, I drew this to me in perfect timing. It was choiceless to continue with Sara in her master's class, as I could not get enough of The Council's teaching and Sara's integration of the teaching.

"After a few months of avid participation, the offer of a channeling class was also choiceless for me. As we learned each week and Sara encouraged us to start journaling, it was effortless and easy for me. As she taught us to go from our heads into our hearts and just write whatever came through, it just flowed, and thoughts and guidance poured onto the page. I started each day on my balcony writing whatever came through my pen after I posed a question at the top of each page: What is my next perfect step? What does my soul want me to know? It was never forced or felt weird, although I did wonder if I was just making it up a few times. I decided to put judgment aside and just let it flow.

"When Sara encouraged us to find a buddy, I immediately felt drawn to two people. One lived in my state, so I reached out to her, and the other lived in my time zone. My encounters with my first buddy were pleasant, but she had to cancel or reschedule almost every time due to unexpected events in her life. She wasn't really committed. When I reached out to my second buddy, we always showed up for our sessions. We were both totally committed to prioritizing the times we chose over any other events. And we found out that just showing up with an open heart to practice and learn from each other was the magic key to success.

"We were both able to schedule three times a week to get together for two hours. We would always start with conversation about Sara and The Council's message and what was going on in our lives. Then we would take turns channeling. We were both open to see what came through with little anxiety, and trusted that our guides would be there for us. And they always were! It was easy and effortless for both of us from the first day, and still is today. We have been practicing for 18 months together, recording every session, and deepening our relationships with our guides—*our Council*—and with one another. Just like anything, playing an instrument, getting a master's degree, building a house, it takes time and dedication. The joy it brings is worth the effort and the investment of time.

"Now after all these months we still meet regularly, and the energy of our guides coming to us and through us is such a pleasure that we seek to do it as often as we can. My advice to new channelers: 1) Practice your automatic writing first to get warmed up in feeling your guides' messages. 2) Find the right buddy who will show up and cherish the experience. 3) Trust that your guides are with you all the time and it is their greatest joy to speak to you and through you. 4) Have fun with it!

"Sara and The Council have changed our lives. We spend as much time in their vibration as possible, immersing ourselves in repeated listening and experiencing of the energy. If you are drawn to this, your guides are waiting for you, and always sending you love."

Practicing with your buddy can take place over the phone, an online video platform, or in person. In person is preferrable, but any of these options will work. Before you begin, discuss who will ask questions and who will practice channeling. Ensure that the person asking questions has a list of questions. Then create a sacred space. You can do this simply by taking a few moments to silence electronic devices or surround yourselves in a circle of light.

If it's helpful, you might ask your buddy to lead you in a guided meditation like the one provided at the end of this chapter. Then your buddy can begin to ask you questions. You might feel most comfortable with your eyes closed, but some channel with their eyes open. Continue with the process of your buddy asking you questions and you tuning in to higher wisdom for the answers.

If you get stuck or feel like nothing is happening, take some deep breaths and focus on going from your head to find the answers, down into your heart, and relax. Allow the answers to come. You might guide your buddy to help you if they notice you might be stuck. Ask them to gently repeat the question a few times until an answer comes through.

As you practice, it will get easier and more fluid. Trust whatever comes through without judgment of yourself or the information. I encourage you to always record your sessions with your channeling buddy and listen back to the replay. You might hear and experience the messages from higher wisdom in a new and unique way.

You might be blown away by what comes through while practicing with a buddy. Many times I've had students who feel like they are not getting messages or that nothing is happening. However, once they find a buddy and start practicing, all of a sudden answers start flowing through them, and their channeling begins to open up in new, exciting ways.

One of my students, a man from North Carolina, describes how important it was for him to get a buddy or channeling partner to practice: "Throughout my experience with Sara's work, I discovered that I am a channel. The benefits of channeling are far beyond just an occasional insight and gut instinct. It took me some time to fully trust myself, but that was because I took a long time to follow the guidance of practicing my channeling abilities with a channel partner or buddy. I have practiced Zen meditation for decades. I've had deep insights and experiences of connection and oneness. However, channeling allows you to go beyond the concepts of connectedness and oneness. Channeling allows you to have direct, firsthand experiences with others that also prove your connectedness and oneness with others in miraculous ways.

Channeling allows you to dramatically accelerate your spiritual journey. You could say it turbo charges your spiritual journey, because instead of getting insights and wisdom from others, you are getting them directly from Source."

If you want to go to the next level, or if you want to explore other ways that might help open and expand your channel, finding a buddy might be the most helpful way for you to do so. If possible, practice with your buddy each week or as often as possible. Most importantly, have fun with it!

GUIDED MEDITATION FOR PRACTICING WITH A BUDDY

This process can be done alone, but it is preferrable to have someone read the following process to you so that you can close your eyes. Find a quiet place where you will not be interrupted, or create a sacred space with your buddy, and then begin.

Let's begin by taking a few deep breaths. Breathing in one, two, three, four, five and breathing out five, four, three, two, one. And repeat, breathing in one, two, three, four, five and breathing out five, four, three, two, one. One more time, breathing in one, two, three, four, five and breathing out five, four, three, two, one. Begin to feel your body get lighter and lighter as you breath in and out, taking deep breaths.

Now imagine a perfectly round hole in the ceiling of the room you are in, and through this hole there is the most beautiful, bright light coming down, coming down through the ceiling above you. It is the brightest, most beautiful light you have ever seen. The whole room is now filled with this light.

Now I want you to imagine the light coming down through the perfectly round hole in the ceiling above you, and it is now moving down into the crown of your head. I want you to imagine an opening in the crown of your head, and this beautiful, bright light is now coming down into the top of your head. Feel the crown of your head opening and expanding as the bright, beautiful light begins to flow into the crown of your head.

Now feel the space on your forehead right between your eyes—your third eye. Feel the space on your forehead right between your eyes opening and expanding. Imagine the bright, beautiful light flowing down from the top of your head into your third eye, the space right above your eyes. Feel the entire area open, expand, and fill with the bright, beautiful light.

Now imagine the bright, beautiful light traveling down through your eyes, over your cheek bones, down through your face and into the area around your throat. Feel the space in the back of your throat opening and expanding. As you feel your throat opening and expanding, imagine the bright, beautiful light flowing down into the area around your throat. Feel the entire area open, expand, and fill with the bright, beautiful light.

Now bring your focus down to your heart. Feel the bright, beautiful light flowing down over your shoulders and your shoulder blades. Feel your shoulders relax. Imagine the most beautiful space within your heart and feel a tremendous opening in your heart. Imagine the bright, beautiful light traveling down into this tremendous opening in your heart and filling you with light. Feel the entire area open, expand, and fill with the bright, beautiful light.

Now imagine the light flowing down through your lungs, your rib cage, and over each one of your ribs. Feel the bright, beautiful light flow into your abdomen, into the space around your belly button. Feel the entire area open, expand, and fill with the bright, beautiful light.

Now imagine the space between your hip bones and your pelvic bones. Feel the bright, beautiful light traveling down into your pelvic area. Feel this area opening as the bright, beautiful light fills this area. Feel the entire area open, expand, and fill with the bright, beautiful light.

Now focus on the base of your spine, near your tailbone. Imagine this area opening and expanding as the bright, beautiful light travels down into the base of your spine and fills this area with the most beautiful, bright light. Feel the entire area open, expand, and fill with the bright, beautiful light.

Now imagine the bright, beautiful light traveling down your thighs into your legs, over your knees, through your shins, down into your feet. Now imagine the bright, beautiful light going through your feet into the floor, into the ground, into the earth beneath you. Feel your whole body filled with light as the bright, beautiful light flows through your entire body, down into the earth beneath you. Breathe in and just feel the bright, beautiful light going through you. Feel how light and vibrant your body feels.

Feel the bright, beautiful light within you, beneath you, above you, and all around you. Feel your whole body filling up the room with light. Now imagine yourself gently releasing your body and floating up with the light in the perfectly round hole in the ceiling. Gently float up and look down at your body and the room beneath you.

Look down at your body sitting comfortably in your chair or lying on your bed. Now float up through the perfectly round hole and look down at the roof of your home or the building you are in. Look down at the top of the building and see the rooftop. Then float up to the tops of the trees and see the tops of the trees, maybe you look down to see people walking, or children playing or animals, maybe you see a bird fly by. Now floating above the trees, go upward to the clouds.

Float up higher and higher until all you see are clouds all around you and gently floating by you. Feel the warm rays of the sun on your face and on your skin, as you float up above the clouds.

Then, begin to look for the perfect cloud. When you find just the perfect cloud, sit down on that perfect cloud, and make yourself comfortable. Sit comfortably on your perfect cloud, above it all. Notice how peaceful and quiet it is here above it all, sitting on your perfect cloud.

At this point, your buddy might begin with their questions, or can continue on with these questions as part of the guided meditation and practice session.

Are you there? When you are there, I want you to ask yourself a question.

Ask yourself the question, *"Who am I?"*

Repeat it again, *"Who am I?"*

If nothing comes, your buddy might ask the question a bit differently and repeat, *"Who are you?"*

Now that you know who you are, ask yourself, *"Why am I here?"* *"Why am I here?"*

If nothing comes, your buddy might ask the question a bit differently and repeat, *"Why are you here?"*

Now ask yourself, *"What is my purpose?"*

"What is my purpose?"

"What is my purpose?"

If nothing comes, your buddy might ask the question a bit differently and repeat, *"What is your purpose?"*

Now ask yourself, *"Who is my spiritual guide or angel?"*

"Who is my spiritual guide or angel?"

"Who is my spiritual guide or angel?"

If nothing comes, your buddy might ask the question a bit differently and repeat, *"Who is your spiritual guide or angel?"*

Now ask yourself, *"What else do I need to know?"*

"What else do I need to know?"

"What else do I need to know?"

If nothing comes, your buddy might ask the question a bit differently and repeat, *"What else do you need to know?"*

When you feel complete, that all questions have been answered, it's time to leave the cloud you are sitting on. Imagine at the end of your cloud a beautiful, lush meadow with green grass and wildflowers appears. Step down off the cloud into the beautiful meadow of wildflowers. You might notice birds or butterflies in the meadow. You might notice trees, mountains, or a lake. Notice what's around you in the meadow of wildflowers.

As you look toward the edge of the meadow, you notice a gate. Begin walking toward the gate. As you walk toward the gate, notice if anyone has appeared and is walking with you in the meadow as you walk toward the gate. Is anyone there with you? Maybe they are walking next to you or maybe they are holding your hand. Keep walking toward the gate.

As you get to the gate, take a moment, and see if there is anything you want to say to this person who is walking with you. Is there anything that they want to say to you? Take as much time as you need with them.

When you are ready say good-bye to them, wave good-bye, or hug them. Then, reach down to open the gate. Notice what the gate looks like and how to open it. Open the gate and walkthrough.

As you walk through the gate, in front of you a staircase appears. What does the staircase look like? Is it a spiral staircase? Is it just brown wooden stairs? When you are ready, start walking down the stairs, stepping down, stepping down. The stairs will lead you back to the treetops, back to the rooftop of your home, back down through the ceiling, and back down into your body. Step down, step down, back into your body.

When you get back down into your body, notice how good your body feels. Begin to feel your hands and your feet. When you feel like you are back in your body, take a few deep breaths, and when you are ready, gently open your eyes.

As earlier recommended, it's best to record these experiences and the answers that come through you. However, this would also be a good time to write down the answers to your questions:

Who am I?

Why am I here?

What is my purpose?

Who is my spirit guide or angel?

What else do I need to know?

Write down anything else that comes to you about your experience. Write down who met you in the meadow and what message they had for you. Write down anything you noticed about your perfect cloud, the meadow of wildflowers, the gate, or the staircase. Write down anything else you noticed or any other messages you received during the process.

As you contemplate the answers to your question, these will serve as powerful tools to help open your channel, trust yourself, and allow higher wisdom.

CHAPTER 10

LIVING THE WISDOM AND GUIDANCE YOU CHANNEL

The best part of channeling is living the wisdom and powerful guidance you receive. Channeling is first and foremost for *you*. It can be fun to share your channeled messages with others. It is also very rewarding to channel professionally for others and offer private sessions or group sessions. However, there are no messages that come through you that are not also *for you* in some way. And the *very best part* is how the wisdom, guidance, and information you receive from higher wisdom changes your life. It is the greatest gift you will ever give yourself. It is the best thing you will ever do for yourself.

One of my students, a woman from Sweden, explains, "To me, channeling is a way of living that opens up and expands our human potential, redefining what being human actually means. It is a way of living that enhances life, making it richer, fuller, and more fun!

"I believe that we are all channeling to some extent every day, and it is just so beneficial to understand how to navigate consciousness. When we remember and embody the pure love that we are, we stand in our power and live in the infinite abundance that is our birthright, that is us. Entering requires radical personal responsibility, and only you know if you are ready. Either way, you are adored! Always."

Every message is for you. When you apply the wisdom and the tools that come from higher wisdom, you can begin to rapidly create more peace, joy, love, connection, well-being, abundance, and freedom in your life. When you allow the loving energy of Source to flow through, you begin to regenerate the cells in your body and rejuvenate well-being. You become a magnet for things that are aligned to the vibration of abundance. Your relationships become more loving, and you feel connected to everything. It truly is a magical and extraordinary way of living when you embody and apply higher wisdom in your everyday life.

I once heard a well-known channel say that the information he channeled was great, but it was more for his followers and not something he applied in his own life. I found myself almost angered by the comment. I thought to myself, Why would someone channel such amazing wisdom and answers to living a better life and then *not* apply the information? I was so triggered that I knew there was something imperative for me about his comment.

I came to the conclusion that I was going to be the ultimate student of the wisdom of The Council. I didn't know it at the time, but this inspired a radical new way of teaching and sharing channeled information. I began to offer my own experiences of how I integrate and live the wisdom as part of my programs and courses. The irony is that some years later, I heard that same channel speak again, and he proclaimed that he had started to apply his channel's wisdom in his own life and was happier than ever.

The very best part is living this and knowing that you're worthy of this higher wisdom that is always aware of you, always guiding you, and always available to you *no matter what*. It is our natural and inherent state to access higher wisdom while having a human experience. We never intended to forget or turn away from the powerful guidance and awareness that was available to us in every moment.

As one of my students from Los Angeles explains, channeling is absolutely an inner compass and a tool that has the power to assist you on a journey that you choose to take. In her experience, it has allowed her into an expanded awareness on things she didn't know even how to ask for or about. Know that there is a force that fully accepts you, assists you, and is always there for you. She shares that channeling has allowed her to "embody full authority in my life and find this loving validation inside me."

Another student, a woman from Lake Tahoe, explains her experience like this: "Before I met Sara and The Council, I'd been channeling for five years, but in a different way. I'd held gatherings and experienced beings who came in to speak as entities outside of me coming to impart their wisdom. It was nice, pretty unconventional, but still, mostly theory, as I took baby steps toward trusting it.

"However, the dimension of channeling I've come into through Sara and The Council is an entirely different experience. It's a full-time romance with Source. The insights come to me, surfacing without my seeking. It is passionate, playful, and it is real. Instead of pen pals, Spirit and I are now so richly sharing a body and beyond.

"The landscape of my life has transformed from a war zone to an ease of Heaven on Earth. Instead of experiencing grief and sorrow in my life, I now bathe everything with my love, no matter what. I can relax into knowing it's only a dream.

"If I had not met this unfoldment of meeting Sara and discovering my relationship with Source, my life could have been suffered away, scorched, and shrunken by buying into the opinions of others. I should add that none of this would have been possible without the support and nonjudgment of my beloved Sara Landon community. Now, because my higher love and wisdom have sparkled into life, I can fulfill the task my soul has chosen—to bring an awakening of divine love in this world."

LIVING IT FOR YOURSELF

Living it for yourself is the most important part. Some of you will feel inspired to share your channeled messages with others or with the world. Many people explain feeling *called* to be a messenger of divine love and light in the world. Some of you will simply enjoy your connection to higher wisdom and not feel the desire to channel for others. That's perfectly fine. Others might want to provide their channeling abilities and expertise to others as a service or a product.

Over the years, many of my students have become professional channels, healers, guides, wayshowers, and teachers since discovering their gifts and abilities. Like any other talent, ability, or gift, we are here on this planet to exchange our gifts with others, and money is a form of exchange. Money is energy, and charging money for your services or abilities is a form of energetic exchange. A woman in my community once asked The Council if it was okay for her to charge money for her spiritual gifts. The Council replied that everyone's gifts and abilities are *spiritual* regardless of their profession. It is perfectly fine to value your gifts, talents, and abilities and request an energetic exchange in the form of money.

There are also many other forms of energetic exchange. You might exchange your channeling talents and abilities with someone who is a beautician, pet sitter, builder, repair person, artist, musician, teacher, or almost any other profession, skill, or talent. There is a woman in my community who does channeled hands-on healing work. With almost all her clients, she finds some mutually beneficial way to exchange healing for things she needs and enjoys. She exchanges healing sessions with a woman who gives facials and does skin care. Another example: She does healing sessions weekly in exchange for rent at the place where she lives. She also exchanges healing sessions for meals with a local restaurant owner.

Others provide their services for donations only. They do not charge a fee but accept donations. Others offer a pay-what-you-can model. All of these are great ways to exchange your abilities and talents. On occasion, a few people have expressed no interest in charging for their channeling works and want to offer their gifts for free. Each person must honor what they feel is right for them or what they are guided to do.

In my own experience, I knew not only the value that my channeling offered to help others change their life, but I also knew my dedication, years of practice, and commitment to creating professional, beautiful, channeled products required an energetic exchange in order to sustain, grow, and expand The Council's wisdom in the world. When you do what you love and are passionate about, it's truly not work. Yet you are worthy of receiving for all that you give. The Council explains that the energy of giving and receiving are one. In all that you give in your passion to bring love, light, and higher wisdom to the world, remember to allow yourself to receive.

You don't have to evolve your channeling abilities professionally and offer services, but many feel the inspiration or desire to do so. Just you *being* in a higher level of consciousness and in a higher vibration is serving in ways that you can never understand. Every message you receive and the energy that flows through is for you. Connect with every message and know it is for you, practice the wisdom, and live it yourself. That's what really changes things in your life!

CHAPTER 11

YOUR LIGHT
IS YOUR
PROTECTION

There are many myths and misunderstandings about channeling. Most result from fear, lack of experience, lack of consciousness, and religious dogma. In this chapter we are going to eliminate the misconceptions of dark forces, dark energies, attachments, rituals needed to protect yourself, and negative entities coming through when you channel. We will expel the myths that channeling is satanic, the devil's work, or demonic. By the end of this chapter, you will understand that channeling is about elevating yourself into a state of pure love and aligning to the unconditional, unwavering love that is within you and always available to you.

When I first started channeling, I didn't fully understand what was happening. I was familiar with trance channeling that occurred when an entity completely took over someone's body, but I didn't know anyone at the time who was a conscious channel, like me. One day, I found myself in the spiritual section of a bookstore and thought I would look for a book about channeling. Much to my surprise, there *was* a book on channeling, only one, written many years ago.

I opened the book to a random page, curious to read more about channeling. I happened to open the book to a page that said something to the effect of, "You've got to protect yourself. There are dark forces and bad entities *out there* that will attach to you and use you for dark forces in the world."

I immediately shut the book, put it back on the shelf, and left the bookstore. The words I read were the complete and total opposite explanation of my experience of channeling. In fact, the way I describe my experience of channeling is that it's the most incredible vibration and energy of pure bliss and unconditional, unwavering, pure love that I had *ever* experienced *anywhere* in my life.

I calculate that I have channeled at least 10,000 hours. I have taken over 5,000 students from around the world through The Art of Channeling process. I have *never* personally or through the experiences of my students had any sort of dark entity come through, dark force try to attach, or negative force take over. I have only experienced the energy, consciousness, and vibration of love when channeling.

To understand the myth of dark forces, we must explore levels of consciousness to understand that negative entities do not exist in *higher levels* of consciousness. Most who are in the human experience are in the 3rd Dimension, which is the dimension of separation. In the 3rd Dimension you experience lack, limitation, fear, suffering, pain, good versus bad, right versus wrong. As you begin to raise your vibration and your consciousness, you will move into the 4th Dimension, which is the dimension of transformation. Here, you begin to understand that you can change your circumstances and conditions. You can heal from the past by elevating yourself and your thoughts—out of the past, out of the old, out of the struggle.

The 5th Dimension is the dimension of pure love. It's what you might call Christ consciousness, unity consciousness, or oneness consciousness. There are also higher dimensions of consciousness beyond physical form where one might describe the experience as pure bliss, being eternal, ever-present, all-knowing, or divine. These are the dimensions we access when channeling and the levels of consciousness where higher wisdom exists.

One cannot be in the 5th Dimension of pure love and experience suffering or fear. One cannot be in the 5th Dimension of pure love and then harm, attack, or abuse another. It is simply impossible to experience what is present and exists in lower-level vibrations and lower levels of consciousness when you are in a state of pure love or higher dimensions.

I believe the collective human consciousness has raised considerably over the last 10, 20, 30, or 40 years, offering a potentially different experience and perspective. It's possible that dark forces or negative entities *did* exist at one time when the collective human consciousness was different than it is now. It's possible that through the evolution of survival the wild animal lurking behind you in the dark became the monster under the bed or the dark forces haunting you from beyond.

It's also possible that the presence of higher beings at one time scared the human that observed them and therefore were considered to be dark forces when perceived by one who was in fear. And then this fear was passed down through generations. It's possible that highly emotional experiences of pain, abuse, or violence experienced by a person in their life influenced their own belief of negative entities, dark forces, or attachments. This could cause a person to experience the reflection of that in realities seemingly outside of themselves. It's also possible that someone could be accessing some level of consciousness while in an ungrounded or unhealed place where they perceive something as dark and as *out to get them.*

There are also examples of mental, physical, and physiological chemical imbalances in the brain that affect what someone is perceiving as reality. I have tremendous love, compassion, and understanding for anyone affected by these altered states. I acknowledge with reverence and respect everyone's experience. It is just not my experience or anything I have seen my students experience.

My experience is only of love. I have channeled nothing but pure love and have experienced nothing but love through the experience of what my students channel. If higher wisdom, guidance, clarity, and truth is your intention—it will be your experience.

Even if there are dark forces out there, if *you* are in a state of pure love, dark forces could not be present in your experience. If you *fill yourself up with all of you* by being present and in your power in the moment, you will elevate yourself to a level of light, love, and consciousness where dark forces could not come *any-where* near you. Fear and negativity simply cannot exist in the vibration of love and consciousness.

There is nothing to protect yourself from unless you believe in dark forces and therefore draw yourself into an experience of perceiving energy as negative or something that can use you in the service of dark forces in the world. When you are aligned within you to the vibration of wholeness, oneness, innocence, and love, you are aligned to higher wisdom, which is *always of love*. When you fill yourself up with *all of you*, all that you are, the truth of you, *that is how you protect yourself*, although there is *nothing* outside of you to protect yourself from. When in a state of pure love, you are fully aligned to your power and truth.

A lovely woman from Canada who was part of The Art of Channeling was involved in a particular healing modality where a heavily weighted part of the two-year curriculum she attended was about how to protect yourself when doing healing sessions. They taught them rituals and techniques to protect themselves. This included protecting themselves from the people they were working with and protecting themselves from *negative attachments* that could *overtake them*. Because she spent two years learning about *protecting herself* from dark energy, she was focused on it, aware of it, concerned about it, and constantly protecting herself throughout her practice, with every client she worked with.

When I explained there were *no dark forces* overtaking her, nothing to protect herself from when she was in her power and aligned to love, she became very angry. I continued to explain that one cannot be in the mindset of believing they must protect themselves from negative forces and also be in their power at the same time. Either you are in the state of consciousness of your wholeness, oneness, perfection, and pure love, or you are in fear, separation, lack, and limitation—where you perceive a lack of your power, wholeness, and love.

After about a week, she came to me and said, "Wow, I had a compete epiphany about how powerful I am! I realize now that if I am focused on negative energy and dark forces, if I am focused on it, and giving meaning to certain things as being dark or able to harm me, that, of course, I need to protect myself, but that's just the experience I was creating."

Rituals and ceremonies are wonderful, beautiful, and can be sacred, but are not necessary to protect yourself unless you believe them to be, or you enjoy the beautiful, sacred experience of creating a ceremonial ritual to honor your channeling practice. There are many wonderful ways to create a sacred space to experience in preparation for channeling and doing healing work. Many people use crystals, feathers, smudging, candles, mantras, and incense to clear and prepare a sacred place. These are all beautiful and wonderful tools. Just realize these things are not more powerful than you. Your intention is what activates these tools, and your own power and love are all you ever need to protect yourself.

What you are focused on and the meaning you are giving it, is what is creating your reality. What you are focused on is what you are drawing to you. If you are focused on something outside of you that could take power over you, hurt you, harm you, then you are in a vibration of fear and powerlessness. This will lower your vibration and your consciousness, where you entangle with lack, limitation, fear, and separation. If you start focusing on dark, bad things and give meaning to those things, you are entangling with them. You get *more* of what you focus on.

When you protect yourself by filling yourself up with all of you, you will know that *there is only love.* Go form your head into your heart and fill yourself up with all of *you.* Not your fears, doubts, stories, but with the real, true, powerful essence of YOU! As you feel yourself filling up with light and love, you are raising your vibration and level of consciousness. You are aligning to higher wisdom, which is always in the vibration of pure love.

Many years ago, I had a session with a woman who argued with The Council that she had been energetically attacked. The Council would not waver in their reply. Over and over in different ways they kept saying, "There is no energy attacking from outside of you in any way. All the energy is *your energy.* If you elevate yourself into the truth that *there's only love* and that everything's happening *for you,* you will come into your power, you will come into *your light,* you will realize that *your power is love.*"

Suddenly, she got quiet. I could hear her voice soften, and felt a shift. She acknowledged that she could now see that she wanted to hold on to the *belief* that it was something *outside of her*. She came back to me after her session and said, "Oh, wow, I had an epiphany after that session!"

It was a belief that she had and a story that she kept projecting into her experience that kept showing up as something energetically attacking her. It was her own beliefs and thoughts about herself that were resulting in her feeling of being attached. She said, "I literally saw how my story was directing energy to play out in a way that it felt like I was being attacked by something." She went on to say, "I got it! I did what The Council said, I elevated myself into love and *light*, and I've never had that experience again." Nothing outside of her seemingly attacked her again.

I once had a neighbor who knows that I communicate with spirit and asked me for help. She wanted me to talk with her daughter who had been seeing ghosts. The mother explained that her daughter was up every night and unable to sleep because she was afraid of ghosts. When I talked with the young girl, she explained that she would see ghosts in her room, and she became so frightened, she couldn't sleep. I asked the daughter what about the ghosts frightened her, and she started to tell me about a scary movie with ghosts that she had seen. When I asked if the ghosts in her room looked like the ghosts in the movie, she said, "No." I asked her if the ghosts in her room had done something to scare her. Again she said, "No, but I just know that ghosts are scary."

I told her next time she saw or felt a ghost in her room, to close her eyes and go into her heart. She asked how to do that, and I said, "Just go from being in your head and focus on your heart." I told her, with her eyes closed tightly, to think of all the things she loved—like her mom, dad, brother, dog, cat, friends, grandmother, anything she loved. I told her to feel her whole heart filling with love as she thought about all the things and people she loved.

Then, I said, "When your heart is completely filled up with love and you have thought about all the things you love, then open your eyes." I said, "If it is *not* a friendly ghost, it will have to go away when you fill yourself up with love." I told her that she was powerful and that her power was *love*.

Almost immediately, she responded and said that she wasn't *really afraid* of ghosts. I could feel the shift from fear to love. A few days later, her mother told me that her daughter was sleeping all through the night and hadn't since mentioned the scary ghosts. Her daughter still experiences visitations from ghosts, angels, or spirits, but she understands her own ability to align with her power and with love.

Protect yourself by filling yourself up with all of you and focusing yourself into a state of love. There is only love. The Council says time and time again, "One of you aligned to your power, in your truth, aligning to the truth of who you are, the love that you are, the divine being that you are, the messenger of divine love that you are, you are more powerful than millions that are not, physical or *nonphysical*."

If there are dark entities *out there*, they could never come anywhere near you, *if* you are in your power, and that power is your love and your light. When you come into alignment through awareness and the elevation of your vibration and consciousness, you open up to Source Energy, you open up to your connection and fully allow it, and you can create worlds.

Most importantly, you create *your own world*. The Source Energy that creates worlds is *in you*. It is that *light* that you fill yourself up with. You are unlimited in your power and ability to align with pure love. Fill yourself up with all of you!

A VISUALIZATION TO FEEL YOUR TRUE POWER

Take some deep breaths and allow yourself to feel the truth within these words. You are the powerful force of divine love in the world. You are the powerful Source Energy in the world. You are the powerful light that shines so bright. You are the power.

Allow your power here and now. Breathe it in. Take a deep breath and feel your power filling up every part of your body, every cell of your body receiving the power that is you as you go into your heart and feel your power.

Feel your power. Feel your power expand to the top of your head and down to the bottom of your feet and out your fingertips. Feel every cell in your body filling with the power of the divine love that you are, filling with the power of the divine light within you, filling with the powerful Source Energy that is you. Feel the power within you, the power that creates worlds, the power that creates your world.

Feel the power within you that anything and everything is possible for you. Feel the power of the truth of who you really are. Feel the power of how important you are. Feel the power of how important it is that you are here in this life here and now, creator of your reality. Feel the power of knowing that you are creator within your own creation.

Feel the power, the powerful I Am Creator frequency that you are. Feel the power that you are, the isness of all that is and all that will ever be. Feel the power. Feel the power of the creator that you are. Feel the power of your sovereignty. Feel the power of the freedom you have to choose and to create your reality anywhere—any way you want it to be.

Feel the power. Feel the power. It's your power. Your power is for you. And as you feel your power and you're expanding from you in every direction the powerful love and light that is you, feel every aspect of your power that has somehow gone somewhere to someone out beyond you. Feel it flowing back to you. Feel the love flowing through you as you allow all of your power to come back to you. Feel the power like nothing you've ever felt before in this moment. Feel all of your power coming back to you. Claim that your power is for you.

Your power is love and your power is here and now. And feel all of your power within you now. Feel the integration of every part of your power flowing back to you. Feel your power flowing back to you. And as you feel the integration of your power within you and you feel the wholeness and completeness of all of your power here in this moment for you, with you, of you, expanding from you; you are the power.

You are the power that creates worlds. You are the powerful I Am Creator frequency. You are the powerful, powerful creator of your reality, creator within your own creation. Feel your power. And as you feel the completeness of all of your power and you feel so deeply into your worthiness to allow your power and to feel your power and to be in your power, know that this power is love, it's kindness, it's truth, it's consciousness, it's freedom, it's harmony within you. Your power feels harmonious. Your power feels blissful. Your power feels peaceful. But your power feels the truth. Your power feels the master within you, the creator within you.

As you feel your power, you know that you are that which you call God. Creator exists within you now, lives within you now. The power is within you now. You are that power. And with this power you can do anything. You are the power. You are the power.

Now feel your power as the brightest light you've ever seen emanating from the core of your being, through you, expanding from you, illuminating the room that you're in, illuminating the home or the building that you're in, illuminating the town that you're in, spreading across the meadows and the hills and the mountains and the rivers and the streams and the oceans, expanding across this entire planet, this entire Earth, being illuminated in the powerful, bright, beautiful light that is you, and that light shining all the way down through the layers of the earth, through the roots of the trees and the crust of the earth, through the center of the earth.

Your power is limitless as it emanates from you across the horizon, across this earth in every direction down, down, down into the core of the earth. Your power emanating from you, illuminating the sky and the Heavens as far as you can see into all of the universe, is your power, is the light shining from you, the power that you are, the love that you are. You are that power and there's nowhere that you are not. You are the light within the Heavens, you are the light in the sky, you are the light of the sun, you are the power of the sun, you are the power of the moon and the sun and the stars, and all of the universe exists within you. That is how powerful you are. You are the power. You are the power that creates worlds, and you are the power that creates your world. And so it is. And so it is. And so it is.

You are the power of divine love in the world. You are the power of divine love in your world. And you are the power that creates divine love everywhere. It is the truth of you. It is the truth of everyone. You are the power of divine love. That is what you are.

Take a deep breath and feel your power. Take a deep breath, feel your power. Take a deep breath, feel your power. From this place you easily, effortlessly, harmoniously draw to you from infinite resources that are always available to you everything, everything that you could ever need and more for the creation of your reality, for the creation of your Heaven on Earth, for the creation of a New Earth that exists within you and around you right here, right now. And so it is.

✳

CHAPTER 12

CARING FOR YOUR BEAUTIFUL CHANNELING BODY

Your body is the magnificent vessel by which you channel Source Energy. Caring for your body is an important part of channeling, especially when you first begin to channel. Channeling can often have the same effect on your body as taking up a new exercise program or physical activity. At first you might be more tired than normal, but once you build your muscles and get stronger, it gets easier, and you experience less fatigue.

Channeling can also be invigorating to your body. Some people feel energized for hours after doing any form of channeling, like how an athlete might feel after making an amazing play while *in the zone*. Everyone's body is in a different state of health, strength, vibration, and frequency. It's important to honor *your body* and what your body needs as you continue to open your channel to more and more higher wisdom and Source Energy.

When I first started channeling, I channeled approximately 45 minutes per day. I noticed I became very tired after channeling and wanted to sleep. So I practiced channeling in the evening. When I was done, I would often go right to sleep. I also noticed that I needed more sleep than normal and would often sleep 12 hours a night. On occasion, I would have the opposite experience and be extremely energized, and stay up long into the night basking in the high vibrations and frequencies I would feel.

As I continued to practice, I noticed that I could channel for longer periods of time, get in and out of channel quicker, and didn't notice the energetic highs and lows so much. The more you channel, the more you will acclimate to the high levels of energy that you experience while channeling. Over time you will integrate these elevated vibrations, and your own vibrational set point becomes higher as well.

After a few years, I worked my way up to channeling six to eight hours a day doing private sessions for clients. It took me only three deep breaths to get in and out of channel. I also noticed it didn't affect my sleep or activity during other parts of the day. Now it's a very normal part of my life and way of being.

Everyone's body experiences and integrates higher vibrational frequencies in different ways. Some people find channeling to be very easy on their body and integrate the frequencies quickly. Other times, the higher vibrations accessed while channeling are healing and upgrading the channeler's body. This might require a change in sleeping patterns, diet, exercise, habits, and lifestyle.

There is no one way you must eat in order to channel. There is no expectation of doing yoga, meditation, using crystals, or becoming vegan. While all those things can be helpful to raise your vibration, they are not a mandatory component to channeling or being spiritual.

There are three things that my own channel, The Council, said are most important for anyone who is channeling. Sleep, water, and play are necessary things to support your body when channeling. Make extra time to sleep and rest if you feel tired. Drink plenty of water. Since I started channeling, I drink approximately a gallon of water per day. This is a primary requirement my body has in order for me to channel for long periods of time and integrate higher vibrations and frequencies.

Play is likely not something you might consider as *a need*, but The Council repeatedly recommends play. Channeling can often become very serious when accessing higher wisdom and your soul. Channeling is a beautiful experience that can be playful and fun. In fact, higher wisdom often has a sense of humor and whimsical expression.

Play, have fun, live a wonderful life! Find time to do more of the things you enjoy. Spend time in nature, listen to beautiful music, take up dance, learn to paint, write poetry, and pursue your passions. They are all wonderful ways to express and experience more Source Energy in your body.

It is vital to honor *your body*. If your body needs to rest, rest. If your body is asking you to spend more time in nature, spend more time in nature. If you feel drawn to different foods, allow your body to tell you what it needs for nourishment. Your body knows what it needs to acclimate these new frequencies.

I find that many students feel drawn to spending more time in nature once they begin to channel. Nature can be very soothing to the body. Oftentimes, the body needs the vibration of nature. This is common and often a supportive practice for those who channel. It can also be a wonderful place to tune in to higher wisdom more easily.

It is also significant to create an environment that is supportive of your higher vibration. This includes a safe, quiet place for you to channel where you will not be interrupted. You might need to find a location where you can be alone or place a note on the door that you are not to be disturbed.

Your environment consists of your home, yard, surroundings, relationships, friendships, family, workplace, job, or business. You are worthy of having friends that are kind to you, loving relationships, a work environment supportive to your well-being, and a home environment supportive to your harmony and happiness. If it's not, know that you are capable of creating environments in all areas of your life that support you in maintaining a high vibration.

You might need to ask for the help you need to make changes or have boundaries in certain areas of your life. As your needs change, it's okay to make those changes. You might need to ask people in your home to allow you uninterrupted time. You might need to ask your friends, family members, or partners for assistance. These are all things to consider as part of caring for yourself and your body.

Over the years, one of the most common questions I receive is about food and what you can or cannot eat in order to channel. Every body is different. I know many channelers who felt guided to a vegan or vegetarian diet once they started channeling. I know an equal number of channelers who felt guided to eat more protein, meat, or fish once they started channeling. In a few particular cases, I know people who were vegan or vegetarian for over a decade that started eating meat as an essential part of caring for their body once they began channeling. There is no right or wrong way for every body.

Honor yourself, honor your body. Whatever it is that you're eating, bless it. It is more important how you feel about what you are putting in your body. Listen to *your body*. The body has a magnificent way of drawing to itself from its environment what it needs to thrive. Your body is intelligent, and it will communicate with you what it needs. As a channel, your most essential job becomes taking care of your vessel, your channel, your body's ability to tune in to those higher vibrations and higher levels of consciousness.

Another student, a wonderful woman from Las Vegas, was journaling and asked her higher self for a message about her body. She was fully expecting the response to be about diet and exercise; instead, the message from her higher self was, "Ask your body." So, she asked her body what it wanted her to know. The response shocked her and brought her to tears: "Please just love me."

The response was so powerful, it felt to her like a beautiful small child pleading to just be loved and accepted after years of neglect, abuse, and being shamed. The wisdom in that message changed everything about her life. It led to her being able to embody unconditional self-love and worthiness, which she says is the foundation for everything. Maybe the most important thing you can do to take care of your body, is to *just love it*.

A Message from The Council on Loving Yourself

We are so pleased and delighted to have the opportunity to speak with you on this fine and glorious day indeed. We assure you all that you are becoming is the truth of your power, your brilliance, your magnificence. You're beginning to open up to the light that is always available to you. The light *is* you. You are the light that shines so brightly in this world. You might already identify with being a bright light in this world and want to shine your light brightly to bring truth and elevate humanity into peace, joy, and harmony. We assure you, that is why you are here.

It is going to be even more fun and enjoyable, and you will love your life even more, our dear friend, as you fully embody all that is possible for you. You are a messenger, a wayshower, an uplifter, a dreamer, a guide. You are here to live your life to the fullest, to love fully, to be all that you are. As you go beyond the limitations of the human experience intentionally, consciously, by opening and allowing, you begin to transcend the struggles, the things that hold you back, the limited thinking, to allowing your life to be everything you meant it to be.

Be gentle on yourself. Enjoy the unfolding. The more you love yourself, the more you love your life, the more you love what you do and how you do it and all that is here for you, the more you begin to open and receive guidance, intuition, gifts, and resources like money, time, and all that you need.

The energy of giving and receiving is one and the same. If you're wanting to fully embrace all that you are here to give, then fully embrace and receive all that is here for you. Do not deny your power. Do not deny that you are worthy of this connection to infinite intelligence that is always available to everyone, if you will allow it.

You are sacred, and every single place on this earth is sacred. Wherever you are is a sacred place. *You* are the one who is focusing on a place that is special to you and giving that place meaning. Therefore, focus your intention in such a way that you give power to these places.

There are certain places that are very thin places, meaning that it's easier to access higher levels of consciousness because of the vibration of that place. High vibrational places have played an important role in humanity's evolution of consciousness. Now, as the more embodied, enlightened master that you are, having realized your power and your potential, that consciousness and vibration is your opportunity. *You* are the one to create sacred spaces, holy ground, and ancient places wherever you go.

You could focus upon a tree in your yard and give it the meaning that it was grown from a seed that belonged to the Master Jesus. It was sent from the cosmos to Jesus; he carried it in his pocket until he found the perfect place that was guided to him by God. It is where he then planted that sacred seed in the ground. Now, the tree that has formed in your yard was that which was from a sacred seed planted by Jesus himself. And if *that's* the way you focused on it, the meaning you gave it, the level of excitement and enthusiasm you had about it, you would have the most magnificent, high vibrational, expansive awakening, incredible experiences in the presence of that tree because of the meaning *you* are giving it.

There are sacred places on this planet that you might find yourself called to at different times of your life. You might find that certain places feel vibrationally expansive to you. Your opportunity on the planet now is for *you* to be the bringer of the consciousness and the vibration. You will be guided to places that have very high vibrations, that are a vibrational match to the frequency you have expanded into. You will feel called to particular places where you have incredible and amazing experiences.

Allow yourself to have those experiences. You will become more aware of your ability to focus your consciousness into any place, location, or geographical location. You might become more interested in things like teleportation and telepathy as you explore high vibrational places. You will become more aware how to focus your consciousness in such a way that you begin to move physical matter along with your consciousness. Amazing things will open up to you. If you are guided to or have interest in a particular place, ask yourself, "What does this place mean to me? What do you want to show me?"

There are many sacred places on your planet. Many of the designs, creation, and building of these places were channeled from higher realms, or built with sacred geometry and codes you may feel resonance with. Most places that you call the *sacred sites* have been used as portals into higher levels of consciousness such that humanity could continue to evolve over time. Some parts of the Earth have higher vibrations or frequencies, where there are portals of energy where you could have spontaneous experiences into higher dimensions of consciousness or what might be called an *awakening.*

Sacred geometry can help you to remember your connection to the universe, and the universe within you. There are times where the sun, moon, and stars align to certain things on your planet that create openings and portals into higher levels of consciousness and vibration. These are portals of potential and possibility, but that do not give your power away to things outside of you.

We would say it as easy as this: Be conscious of when you are unconsciously holding yourself in lack and limitation. Gently notice those moments. Be kind to yourself. Don't judge yourself. Be conscious and present. Put some love around yourself. Put some light around yourself. Drop into your heart. Open and allow. And then let the energy and the light guide the way. It will be so much easier, more effortless, and harmonious for you.

We are always with you. We are always available to you. You are everything you wish to be. You already are. It is all within you and it always has been. We love you, we love you, we love you. And with that, we are complete.

CHAPTER 13

TOOLS FOR EASY AND INSTANT CONNECTION

Channeling can become so much easier when you have a few helpful tips and tools to connect, especially when connecting to your soul team and guides. When I first began channeling, it took me approximately 15 minutes to get into channel. I would close my eyes and essentially meditate until I felt the energy of The Council.

During one of these experiences, I started to say, "pure bliss, pure bliss, pure bliss," as those were the words that described the energy I was feeling. After the third time of repeating the two words, I could feel The Council's energy come through, and I began to channel. I wondered if it was just a coincidence or if maybe these words could summon The Council again.

The next time I went to channel, I sat down in a comfortable, quiet place, took some deep breaths, repeated "pure bliss" three times, and much to my surprise, instantly The Council came through. It was as if these were the magic words to initiate my connection with them. From that point on, I realized I could use these words at any time to open my own channel for higher wisdom to come through.

As I continued to channel, I realized that they often repeated a particular and unusual phrase. "You are everything you wish to be; you already are." One day when reading out loud some automatic writing I had done, I read, "You are everything you wish to be," but by the time I got to "you already are," I was completely and totally in a channeled state. Still to this day, if I say those words, I will be in a channeled state before I finish the sentence.

A funny sidenote to that—in 2022, I published my first book, *The Wisdom of The Council*. When I went to the studio to record the audiobook, I discovered I could not repeat that phrase out loud without going into channel. As soon as I started to read the sentence, I could feel the energy of The Council come through, and my voice and cadence would change.

If you watch or listen to verbal channels, you might notice that many start the same and end the same way. The Council always begins a channel with, "We are so pleased and delighted to have the opportunity to speak with you on this fine and glorious day." They always end with the same words, "We love you. We love you. We love you. And with that, we are complete."

I have a student who is a beautiful verbal channel of higher wisdom. When she begins a channeling, the way she initiates the connection with her guides is by saying, "Welcome." She might repeat the word 5, 10, or 20 times before the channeled information begins coming through her. This is a normal experience. She has learned to simply repeat the word until she feels the full connection to her channel and then her channeled messages begin to flow through.

These trigger words or phrases can become very helpful when learning how to easily get into a channeled state. It might be a word, phrase, or multiple sentences. Ask your channel to give you a trigger word or phrase to initiate the connection. Once you receive a word or phrase, repeat it out loud or in your head until you feel the opening of your channel and the energy coming through you.

One of my students felt as if she wasn't getting an answer to her request for a trigger phrase. I heard the words, "Go higher. Go higher. Go higher." I asked her to repeat these words out loud over and over, even if it was 100 times, until she felt the connection with her channel begin to flow through. She repeated the words out loud and within about 30 seconds, she began verbally channeling.

You can also consider a mantra like this that helps you to open your channel. When you are in a high vibrational state, like during meditation, what words would you use to describe the way you feel? Some might describe their experience as pure bliss, which is why I believe I was guided to those words. You can use any words that come to you to elevate your own vibration to meet the higher vibration of your guides and soul team.

In time, you might find that you don't need a trigger phrase or mantra anymore. You might also notice that the initiation to open your channel can be done through breath and tuning your focus toward your channel. When I channel now, I simply take three deep breaths and The Council begins. For me, it is always and exactly three breaths. By the time I reach the third breath, I feel as if I am floating in the clouds and in a state of pure bliss, and instantly the channeled messages begin to flow.

These tips are helpful for any kind of channeling. If you are interested in learning to verbally channel, these mantras and phrases can be especially helpful. Verbal channeling can be done on one's own or with a buddy or group of people who ask questions while you channel the answers.

If you want to practice verbal channeling on your own, I recommend you get a voice recording device or use a voice recording application. For some, it is also helpful to use headphones to block out external noise to help focus on channeling. Find a comfortable, quiet place, turn on the recording device, and begin to take some deep breaths. Then, repeat your mantra or phrase over and over.

Be gentle on yourself, allow yourself to relax, and repeat the mantra until you start to feel your vibration rise and your channel opening. Then, *just go!* Start saying out loud anything that comes to you. Don't worry if you think you are making it up. Just keep going. Allow the words to flow through you. It might be a couple sentences, or it might be 45 minutes.

It's common for the energy to just stop. This is true for automatic writing and verbal channeling when there is not someone asking questions to you while in channel. Trust what comes through and keep going. When the energy recedes and the message stops, then it's complete. Go back and listen to the replay. I might also suggest that you have your verbal channeled messages transcribed and read them back to yourself.

If it feels like nothing is happening, you might just say out loud, "I am so happy and grateful. I am so happy and grateful. I am so happy and grateful." This will begin to focus your mind and raise your vibration. As you continue to practice, you will reach a level of consciousness where it becomes very easy to access and open your channeled connection to higher wisdom. So, practice, practice, practice.

I have a member of my Masters Class community who never had any desire to channel. She heard me tell a story about how early on I practiced voice channeling using a voice recorder. One day, she sat down and said, "What does my soul want me to know? What do my team, my guides want me to know?" She then turned on a voice recorder and took a few deep breaths. Much to her surprise, the answers started to flow through her. She channeled an entire 45-minute message from a collective of soul beings. It was really powerful! That was her first experience, and she still does it to this day. If you will allow it, higher wisdom can and will flow through you with effortless ease.

I do not believe that my own channeling would be where it is today if I did not have someone to practice with consistently when I first started channeling and then to have people ask questions of The Council during private and group sessions. This is why I strongly encourage everyone to find a buddy to practice with so they can experience allowing channeled answers and information to come through them.

When I sit down to channel for myself now, I find that it's very different. Most often, I realize that I have no questions, which is how *I know* I am in a channeled state. I hear the words, "All is well." I often sit in that energy for 10 to 15 minutes and there are no words at all. I feel like everything is *known* there in that moment. I feel oneness with everything. There are no questions, just an endless awareness of a higher perspective. I know that I am channeling Source Energy in every cell of my body.

If you want to go to the next level or if you want to explore other ways that might help open and expand your channel, find a buddy. Practice every week. Practice as often as you can. You will be blown away by how easy it is.

I've experienced many times where someone feels they aren't getting messages or aren't able to channel higher wisdom—until they find a buddy and their buddy starts asking them questions. Suddenly, answers from higher wisdom start flowing through them and they realize they *can* channel, and it's easy.

Remember, trust yourself. You are not making it up! Once you know your connection is always there for you, and you have these helpful tools to open your channel, all that's left to do is practice and have fun with it. Before long, channeling will begin to transform your life in the most amazing ways!

CHAPTER 14

MEDITATION AND RAISING YOUR VIBRATION

Meditation has many benefits, like calming your nervous system, improving your mood, and bringing you into greater feelings of peace. Meditation is simply a practice of focusing on clearing one's mind using a combination of mental and physical techniques so that you can achieve mental clarity, emotional well-being, and a present state of awareness and attention. An individual might use the technique of closing their eyes, focusing on their breath, and sitting quietly for a period of time. Others might focus on a particular object, mantra, or visual. There is no wrong way to meditate.

Meditation can also open one's awareness to higher vibrations and frequencies. When you quiet the busy mind and come into the present moment, you naturally raise your vibration. To access higher wisdom, one must raise one's vibration to come into resonance with the vibrational frequencies of beings in higher consciousness.

When I first began channeling The Council, I was guided to begin a daily meditation practice where I would sit quietly for 15 minutes and just focus on my breath. I did not use any formal technique or have any prior experience of meditating. At first, my mind would race. I would think of all the things I needed to get done that day. I felt anxious and would often look at the clock to see how much time was left so I could go off and get things done. It took several weeks for me to begin to feel the state of inner peace and calm so often associated with the practice of meditation.

Eventually, I came to enjoy my morning meditation practice. As I did, I started to notice my vibration increased and I began to feel states of bliss, oneness, and connection. It was in these states that I began to receive downloads of information and feel the presence of higher wisdom. It became an important part of raising my vibration and frequency to fluidly channel The Council.

I meditated consistently for many years. Once I began doing private sessions and channeling several hours a day, I no longer felt the need to meditate, as I was in higher vibrations all throughout the day. I know many channels who meditate and many who do not. While it can be a wonderful tool to access higher vibrations and frequencies, it is not a requirement to channeling.

I encourage students to explore meditation as one way to raise their vibrations and open to higher wisdom. If you have never meditated or prefer not to, I recommend one easy practice that might be helpful. Find a comfortable place where you can sit quietly. Turn on an alarm or timer for five minutes. Then, take three deep breaths and visualize going from your head down into your heart. When you get into your heart, just breathe comfortably in and out until your alarm or timer lets you know the five minutes is up. It's an easy way to raise your vibration in a short amount of time.

There are many ways one can elevate one's vibration, frequency, and consciousness. The Council tells us that the most powerful way to raise your vibration is to simply focus on joy, do the things that bring you joy, and feel your way into a state of joyfulness. This, too, is a practice. One can use joy to instantly come into a place of allowing higher vibrations. Ask yourself, "What brings me joy?" Then, allow your mind to focus on the things that bring you joy. I recommend making a list of at least three things that really bring you the most joy. You might also ask that question of what brings you joy and then allow yourself the time to go do whatever it is that brings you joy. Joy is a very high vibrational state of being.

Gratitude and appreciation are also wonderful ways to raise your vibration. You can do this right now by focusing your attention on what you are grateful for in this moment. Say to yourself, "I am so happy and grateful for . . ." It might be your children, dog, cat, friend, spouse, sunshine, beautiful weather, nature, or a delicious meal. You might also make a list of 10 things you are so happy and grateful for in your life. If you make gratitude a practice for raising your vibration, you begin to appreciate the simplest things and feel a greater sense of fulfillment.

Love is another way to raise your vibration. You might think of the people in your life that you love the most, the things you love, or places you love to visit. Bring them to mind and then focus on really feeling love in your heart. If a particular person or pet comes to mind, let yourself feel as if they are there with you right now and you are enjoying a deep moment of love together. You might notice a feeling of expansion, happiness, or openness. It's also important to focus on your own self-love to maintain and increase your vibration.

Exercise, such as walking, jogging, biking, hiking, doing yoga, or dancing, is another great way to raise your vibration. A consistent routine of exercise or yoga helps to heal, restore, balance, and strengthen your body. Our bodies are an important component of our vibration, and exercise can quickly elevate the body's frequency.

Nature is inherently highly vibrational, and many people describe feeling most connected to spirit when out in nature. This is due to the naturally high frequency of the trees, birds, butterflies, animals, plants, and flowers. You might enjoy a nice walk in nature or sit on the grass and feel the earth beneath your feet. Connect with the birds, flowers, land, and natural surroundings simply by focusing on all the things around you. You might even place your attention on the clouds gently floating by overhead.

A helpful practice to connect with nature is to go sit or lie down on the grass. Close your eyes and feel your body melting into the earth. Feel the entire earth beneath you, supporting you, holding you. Focus on the earth beneath you and begin to feel into the roots of the trees, all the way through the layers of the earth, until you feel your energy flowing all the way down into the center of the earth. Feel that the entire earth is here nurturing, nourishing, and caring for you.

One of my students, a lovely woman from Florida, was walking in the woods and thinking about consciousness, when she saw a piece of a dead tree lying on the forest floor. She put her hands on the seemingly dead tree and asked, "Do you still have consciousness?" She immediately felt a vibrating voice within her say, "Of course, silly girl. Only you humans believe in death!"

Other ways to raise your vibration include listening to a beautiful piece of music or playing a musical instrument, watching a funny movie, eating healthy high-vibrational foods, spending time with positive people, writing, reading, doing something fun or creative, and clearing your space. Once you develop a higher vibrational set point, you will find it easier to connect to higher wisdom and your own intuition. Remember to have fun and do what brings you joy!

A VISUALIZATION TO OPEN TO INFINITE INTELLIGENCE

Take a deep breath. Allow yourself in this moment to come fully into your power. Breathe your power into all of your being. Breathe in the love that you are. Breathe in all that you are. Go within you. Find the still, quiet place of infinite power within you. Feel it. Feel deeply into that place.

As you feel into that place, begin to feel that infinite power within you expanding. Feel it expanding and getting even brighter. Feel it getting brighter as you go deeper and deeper. Feel the infinite power within you beginning to shine now like the brightest light you've ever seen within you. Feel it shining up to the top of your head and down to the bottom of your feet and out your fingertips. Feel the infinite power of the bright, beautiful light within you shining so deeply, so brightly, so boldly in every cell of your body. Shine your bright, beautiful light through every cell of your body, activating every cell, activating every molecule in your body, activating every part of you.

Now expand the bright, beautiful light that is you one foot around you in every direction, above you, below you, beside you, in front of you, behind you. Focus the infinite power within you into this bright, beautiful light that is you, focusing through you one foot around you in every direction. And now fill this room with the bright, beautiful light that is you. Focus this infinite power that is you and fill this room with the bright, beautiful light of you.

Now expand that bright, beautiful light to fill up your whole home with the bright, beautiful light that you are. Now expand that light around your home, up, up, up toward the clouds above the trees, up to the birds. Focus the bright, beautiful light that you are up above you. And now focus the bright, beautiful light that you are down, down, down into the earth beneath you, into the roots of the trees beneath you, down into the center of the earth. And expanding up higher again, above the clouds, up toward the moon and up toward the sun and up toward the sky. Higher, higher toward the stars above you as far as you can see throughout all of the universe. Reaching up, reaching up, shining the infinite power of the bright, beautiful light that you are.

Now go deeper, deeper, deeper into the earth beneath you. Now expand from you in every direction, to the right, to the left, in front of you, behind you, expand this bright, beautiful light that you are all around this planet, all around at this beautiful Earth. Shine the infinite power of the bright, beautiful light all around you in every direction until there's nowhere that you are not in all of the universe. The power of infinite power within you, the power. You are the infinite power, the power. You are the infinite power, the power. You are the infinite power.

Let this bright, beautiful light you shine from within you to every corner of this universe and beyond. Focus it until there is nothing but light. And you are here within the center of your universe, the light that you are, the power that you are. Oh, it's time to shine. It is time to shine and realize that you are your greatest creation, expanding this bright, beautiful light that you are, expanding your infinite power. Coming fully into this moment, knowing that you are the most beautiful creation. You are your most important creation. You are your greatest creation. It is you.

As you stand in this moment shining the bright, beautiful light that you are, allowing your infinite power to radiate from you, fully allowing the Source Energy that flows through you, fully allowing the Source Energy that is you, fully allowing the Source Energy that is all here for you. Focus this bright, beautiful light that you are into everything, into the ground beneath you, into the earth beneath you. Focus this bright, beautiful light that you are into the grass and into the trees and into the birds and into the bees. Focus this bright, beautiful light that you are into the animals, into the trees and the flowers and the mountains and the rivers and the streams and the oceans. Focus this bright, beautiful light that you are into the air that you breathe. Focus this bright, beautiful light into every human heart. Focus this bright, beautiful light that you are into every human heart. Focus this bright, beautiful light that you are into oneness with everything. Focus this bright, beautiful light until you feel yourself into the isness of all that is and will ever be.

Feel the infinite power that you are and infuse it into bright, beautiful light. And as you radiate it from you and feel your way into oneness with everything, you are the isness of all that is and will ever be. It is all here. It is all Source. It is all you. You are your greatest creation. You are your greatest creation. You are your greatest creation. And so it is.

Now go beyond. Go so deeply into this moment that you access every dimension of consciousness, that you feel into everything that is here until you can feel yourself into everything, every dimension, every level, every level of creation within every level of consciousness. Go beyond. Go beyond. And bring all that you are and all of creation and all of the power of the Source Energy within you into this moment and go deeper.

Go beyond. Go into the realization of all that you are beyond what you have believed yourself to be. Go beyond. Go beyond what you have believed yourself to be. Come into the awareness of you as creator. Feel yourself moving into the I Am Creator frequency.

Feel yourself as creator of everything. Feel yourself as creator everywhere. Feel yourself as creator within all eternity. Go beyond. Go beyond. Go beyond to the source of the light. Go beyond. Go beyond the light. Go to the source of the light. Go beyond into all of creation and feel it within you. Go beyond. Go as far as you can feel. Expand into it all. And as you do you realize you are your greatest creation in all of the universe. You are your greatest creation in all of the universe. You are your own greatest creation. And so it is.

Now come back into your body and take a deep breath and feel your body. Feel the light that is still within you. Feel the energy that still flows through you. Take a moment and really, really feel for the truth of this. You are your own greatest creation. You are magnificent. You are radiant. You are brilliant. You are divine.

CHAPTER 15

LIGHT LANGUAGE

As mentioned earlier, Light Language is a cosmic language known and understood by the soul, but uncommon to any language on Earth. It is channeled communication of sounds, frequencies, and light from higher realms for the purpose of healing, awakening, and transformation. It might be described as intuitive singing. To many people, it sounds similar to chanting or speaking in tongues.

Many of my students have experienced a spontaneous onset of speaking Light Language. Most are unfamiliar with it but have an unexplainable knowing of its origin. Each of my students that speaks Light Language has their own unique journeys and uses their gifts in different ways. Two particular students have shared their remarkable experiences with me. Both were former corporate professionals, mothers, *normal people* who had never heard of Light Language, let alone thought they would be doing Light Language for others or as a profession.

One of my students, a woman from Georgia, explains how Light Language changed her life: "I had never heard of Light Language in 2016 when I experienced it for the first time during a Sound Healing Session with a friend who spoke Light Language. During the session, she started to express unusual tones and a seemingly unfamiliar language that was fluid for her.

"I was intrigued by the sound! It felt familiar and I experienced a strange feeling of wanting to reply to her as she spoke it. We talked briefly after the session, and she told me that what I had heard was a Light Language channeling transmission.

"The next morning, I was lying in bed with my dogs. I sat up rubbing the dogs and talking to them, and suddenly this strange language started flowing out of my mouth, like I had been speaking it my whole life! For me, this was such a safe and pure place for it to come through while with my loving animals.

"I felt light, magic, love, compassion, and everything beautiful all at once. I was in tears and awe. It was beyond anything I had ever experienced in my life. I had chills all over my body.

"It continued transmitting in my head even when I was not actually speaking it for weeks and months. I only shared it with a close friend. She, too, felt the power, love, and magic of this Light Language, and we 'played' with it often. We shared the energies we felt and insights that we would receive about a particular subject if we set a specific intention.

"From that point forward, I was obsessed with books and articles to find out more about this thing called Light Language. I learned and truly felt the knowing that the Light Language flowed directly from a soul level deep in the heart, bypassing our busy brains. Our souls speak Light Language fluently! It is pure love.

"When I met The Council channeled by Sara Landon in 2017, they shared that Light Language is their language and explained that it is how they communicate as light beings. They also shared that I had been sharing Light Language Codes through my art, which had begun in 2011. This all felt like a dream come true! I had something magical inside me that I could bring forward at will that filled my heart up to overflowing and brought such joy to others.

"Since that time, I have shared my Light Language with individuals and groups. I have found that it transmits joy, wisdom, love, and so much more to all who hear it. I've also learned through Sara's teaching that this gift is first and foremost for me. It has opened my heart to a whole new level of the magic and love available to me.

"I experience various energies as I channel, and have a deep knowing that Mother Mary is always present. Her light is indescribable. In group transmissions everyone receives exactly what is perfect for them. In the same group, individuals will receive the transmission in a completely different way. The language and tone changes as different energies transmit.

"They usually start transmitting as a joyous welcome and invitation to play. It's difficult to express the joy I feel at these times. Often the transmission will shift to a serious, seemingly ancient energy, and I can feel deep wisdom flowing through my heart. A transmission always ends with an energy of a beautiful loving blessing that also cannot be expressed in words. I am forever grateful that this gift of channeling Light Language has opened through my heart. It has enhanced my life, and I know it will keep expanding as I grow and expand into all that I am."

Another student, a woman in California, shares her remarkable story of using Light Language for healing: "After 20 years working in the corporate world, I never thought I would be someone channeling Light Language or giving energy healing. Light Language came through me spontaneously during a meditation. I felt an energy come down through the top of my head and land in my heart. It felt like something unlocked. As I was speaking it, I felt emotions arise in my body and a feeling of coming home. It felt familiar, as if I've been speaking it for thousands of years and it suddenly awoke within me.

"I never heard it before, so I started googling and researching. I found that many people channeled Light Language. After the activation, I started channeling Light Language in my meditations, and a couple of times it came through during a coaching healing session that I offered to clients. I was scared to speak it in front of others in fear that I would be judged or looked at as a crazy person.

"This fear and doubt in myself shifted after an amazing Shamanic healing session I had with a client. This was a distant healing session, so it was done on a Zoom call. Before we started on the healing session, my client told me that she may be distracted because she had her young boy (he was about four years old) with her. She explained that he had autism so he couldn't sit still. She also mentioned that he didn't speak at all except for a few muffled sounds.

"I wasn't planning to channel Light Language, as that was something I only did with a handful of clients. I wasn't ready to put it out there in the world. I didn't really know how people would react to it, and I wasn't fully confident speaking it in front of others.

"We started the session with a meditation and an aura and chakra cleanse. Her son was not settled yet. He was walking around and climbing on the bed, but I saw that she was able to relax, so I continued. As I started our Shamanic healing journey, I started to feel an energy building within me and moving up to my throat, and the Light Language started to come out. I had my eyes closed and felt myself channeling the Light Language in a powerful way. I felt the energy move all around me and through me. It was very playful and loving. I fully let go and surrendered to it. This went on for about 30 minutes, and then I finished the healing.

"I opened my eyes and saw that her son settled down and was laying down beside her. As with all my clients, I opened the call for feedback and discussion. My client started to cry. She said that when I started speaking this ancient language (this is how she described it), her son stopped moving around and walked up to the screen and was talking Light Language back to me.

"Their audio was muted, and I had my eyes closed during that time, so I didn't see this when it was happening. She said that she had never heard her son speak so clearly and has never seen him so focused. She paused and just sat there looking at him with tears streaming down her face. I was absolutely in awe and so touched.

"In that moment, I felt the indescribable power of channeling. I felt a surge of energy in my body and a confirmation that this was a great tool for healing. How incredible was that?

"The young boy recognized the sounds because his soul recognized it. This activated something within him. The next day she reached out to me and told me that he was able to sleep through the night (which he normally doesn't). Since that day I don't question what comes through me. I now trust when I feel the transmission coming through. I surrender to it, knowing that I am meant to share it with the world, and it is meant to activate another beautiful soul."

Anyone can open to Light Language and discover its benefits for themselves. Now that you are aware of Light Language, you might explore it more and allow yourself to feel for the vibrations and frequencies it transmits. For some, just the awareness of Light Language introduces spontaneous transmissions of it.

Light Language is a powerful form of channeling that has become quite common. It's normal for your brain to want to understand what is being communicated, but remember, the beauty of Light Language is that it circumvents the limitation created by the human mind. Like other forms of channeling, just have fun with it and allow the magic of it to present itself to you.

AN ACTIVATION FOR OPENING TO LIGHT LANGUAGE

Let's begin by going deeper into the light, into the love, into the oneness with All That Is. Take a deep breath. There is nothing for you to do but be here now in the light that is within you and the light that surrounds you. Gently let go, relax, fall into the Isness of All That Is, floating deeper and deeper into yourself. Feel into the harmonious expansion that is here for you *now*.

Begin by imagining infinite, unwavering, pure love coming from within you like a light coming in through the center of the Earth, up, up, up through the roots of the trees and the crust of the Earth, into the bottom of your feet, beginning to rise through your ankles, over your knees, up your legs, into the base of your spine. A light becoming so bright now as it moves from the base of your spine all the way up, all the way up through your heart. Going all the way up, all the way up to the crown of your head, and now expanding into every cell of your body and out your fingertips until your whole body is illuminated in love, in light, in pureness, in oneness.

Now imagine the most beautiful bright light coming down, coming down from the sun, from the sun. The brightest light coming from the sun, flowing gently into the crown of your head, down over your cheekbones, into your throat. Feel the bright, beautiful light flowing over your shoulders, down into your heart, through your rib cage, through your abdomen, down into the base of your spine. The brightest, most beautiful light now flows into the base of your spine, over your hip bones, down to your knees and into your feet, and expanding, expanding into every cell of your body until you can feel the bright, beautiful light illuminating your hands, your hands illuminated in the bright, beautiful light.

Now imagine from every corner of this Earth and every corner of the Universe a wave of pure love, a powerful wave moving toward you from every corner of the Earth, from every corner of the Universe. The wave of pure love is moving toward you, coming closer and closer as it flows into your heart like a gentle wave crashing on the beach. It splashes into your heart, and pure love flows into every cell of your body.

As the wave moves through you and pure love moves into every cell of your body you now feel the wave of pure love moving through your spine, flowing out of you, all around you, while fully immersed in the wave of pure love. And as you are filled from every direction with love and light, you are full and filled up in your wholeness, your completeness, your perfection, overflowing with light and love, illuminated in the light and fully receiving of pure love, filled so full your being overflows.

And now you send out the love, send out the light like an invisible wave of the most powerful energy, an invisible wave of the most powerful energy radiating from you into the ground, through the grass, into the roots of the trees, going high into the trunks of the trees, moving into the air, flowing into breath, breathing it in as humanity breathes in the pure love and light of all that you are and All That Is flows into its being, and the light and the love is now everywhere within it, all around it, the light and the love is everywhere in nature, within all of nature and all around.

Within everything, through everything there is light, there is love. There is peace within you, there is peace all around you, and there is peace on Earth. There is light within you, there is light all around you, and there is light on Earth. There is love within you, and love all around you, and there is love on Earth.

Now imagine all of that love and light like a sparkling particle of infinite creation. And now that sparkling particle of infinite creation becomes an infinite number of sparkling particles of infinite creation going out from your being, sprinkling this entire Earth with potential and possibility, sending out the sparkling particles of infinite creation and pure potential into every corner of this Earth and beyond into every corner of this Universe.

Now allow your soul to infuse within every particle of infinite creation the fulfillment of your destiny. Become so radiant, so radiant, so bright, so full of light, shining in all of your glory, that those particles of infinite creation come flowing to you, are drawn to your radiance, moving toward you from every corner of this Universe. Every particle of infinite creation infused with your highest potential, infused with your soul's desire, infused with your destiny, moving toward you in the form of energy and consciousness, moving into form, moving toward you as particles of infinite creation that are now taking form as the fulfillment of your soul's desires.

Moving into your experience fully now. See the highest vision for your existence moving into form and flowing into your reality now. See your destiny, already in form, moving into your experience, moving into your reality. Particles of infinite creation taking form all around you.

Let your destiny come to you. There is nothing for you to do as your soul's desires move through true creation into your experience. There is nothing for you to do as the highest vision for your existence is revealed to you. Let it be revealed to you now in the light, in the love, in the sparkling particles of infinite creation now in form, the form of your highest potential, the highest vision for your existence, in the form of your soul's desires, in the form of your destiny. Let it move fully into your experience, and let it move fully through you.

Notice the place in which your destiny enters. Is it flowing in through your heart? Is it flowing in from the crown of your head? Let it come from the crown of your head all the way down into your heart as it moves fully through beingness into reality, from reality into beingness as you remember that you are the bright light and pure love. You are the bright light and pure love. You are pure love and you are a powerful creator. You are a powerful creator because you are. You are God, consciousness, the energy that creates everything.

Take a deep breath. This powerful activation is going to draw to you your highest potential, the highest vision, your soul's desires, your ultimate destiny of abundance, prosperity, well-being, love, joy, peace, beauty, freedom. The freedom to experience a joy and a love and an abundance you have never known before.

There's nothing for you to *do*. It is done. It is here. It is now. All That Is asked of you is to receive and be the bright light that you are, to receive and be the pure love that you are, to receive and to be. You are the Isness of All That Is, the I Am Creator frequency.

This is the activation of the I Am Creator frequency that flows through you and out from you like an invisible wave that gathers the particles of infinite creation through consciousness and energy and love and presents to you the highest vision for your incarnation in form, as your reality, as truth.

CHAPTER 16

ANIMAL COMMUNICATION

Imagine being able to understand your beloved pet, receive messages from animals in nature, or reconnect with an animal companion on the other side. Animal communication has become one of the most sought-after forms of channeling in the world. Animal communication helps people understand and communicate with animals, to better understand their behavior, experience, and perspective.

Animals can communicate how they are feeling and what they are thinking through language, pictures, smells, emotions, and physical sensations. An animal might present a mental image or picture to explain its perspective. Others might direct an animal communicator to pain they are experiencing in their bodies through a sensation then felt in the animal communicator's body. Some animals are very fluent in language and will deliver their messages verbally or through automatic writing just like people.

Like all other forms of channeling, some people have a natural, inherent knowing of their gift, while others might discover their gift through spontaneous or divinely orchestrated experiences. Some people have no idea they can communicate with animals until they begin to focus their awareness on connecting with animals and practice with a buddy, just like verbal channeling.

I had never considered myself one who communicated with animals naturally. I found automatic writing and verbal channeling were things that came to me very easily. I have met many gifted and amazing animal communicators over the years, many who have been in The Art of Channeling. I often relied on their abilities to give me messages from my animals, both living and on the other side, instead of discovering my own ability to channel my animals.

I began exploring my own animal communication abilities the same way I did automatic writing to receive a message from a loved one on the other side. My first communication was with my beloved dog, who was like a child to me. He had passed over, and I desperately wanted to hear from him. So I sat down at my desk, took out some paper and pen, and asked him to please give me a message. Immediately, without any hesitation, I began to write. But much to my surprise, I was typing his message on my computer, instead of my normal experience of handwriting. The message came through with such intensity that I stopped looking at the screen and only at my fingers as I typed.

When the message was complete, I felt my dog's energy recede. I looked up at my computer screen. Surprisingly, the entire message was written out with not a single space between words. I had never experienced any message like that, and immediately began to laugh. It was his way of reminding me not to take this all so seriously, which was part of his message to me.

After I went back through the entire typed message, putting the appropriate spaces between words, I read the message out loud to myself. It was perfect. It was just the message I needed to hear of how he was always with me yet playing and having the most magical time on the other side, and he reminded me to do the same here. After that experience, I asked him if we could write his messages by hand and use spaces between the words. He agreed, and I continue to channel messages from him and my other beloved animals who have transitioned.

Years later, I adopted a feral barn cat who was pregnant with kittens. She was frightened of humans and would never allow anyone to touch her. We had to use a humane trap to safely capture her and transport her to my home to have her kittens. She was not mean, just scared. I tried endlessly to gain her trust and for her to allow me to pet her. After several weeks, she was still very scared and hid under the bed most of the time.

One night, very late, I was sitting alone with her. I used the process explained above and dropped into my heart. I showed her how much I loved her and her kittens. She seemed to be receiving my communication, so I showed her an image of me holding her in my lap and petting her. Instantly, and much to my surprise, a song came to my head. It was Elvis's song "Can't Help Falling in Love." I wasn't an avid fan of Elvis's music, but I was pretty certain it was one of his songs. I didn't really know the words except for a couple of verses.

"You want me to sing that song?" I asked her. I got an immediate, "Yes." So I began to sing to her over and over the couple of verses that I knew of the song. She started to purr, came out from under the bed, cautiously walked over to me, and started rubbing her head on my leg. I couldn't believe my eyes. I just kept singing the verses I knew over and over. After a few minutes, I reached down and began to pet her. I continued doing this every evening until one night, while singing, I sensed that she was ready for me to hold her in my lap. I showed her the image and immediately felt her sense of comfort. I reached over and gently picked her up. She was completely calm, snuggled up on my lap, and began to purr.

She is now the most loving, affectionate cat. I continue to communicate with her, and she now talks back quite easily, so I no longer use images. She tells me how happy she is to be here with me and her two kittens that we also adopted. I truly believe that learning to communicate with her is what has allowed her to trust me and find the confidence to overcome her fear of humans.

You can start communicating with animals at any time and with any animal you wish. It does not have to be a pet. You might feel drawn to communicate with animals in nature or even the collective of an animal species, like asking for a message from the lion consciousness. Take your time, drop into your heart, and trust the answers and messages you receive.

One of my students from Ontario, Canada, shares how she has become a channel for both people and pets. Here is her story and guidance for others who wish to channel animals:

Sara says there's a moment in every channel's life when we shift from trusting to truly knowing our channelings are genuine. For me, that moment was when I listened to a channeling that I had done of a dog who had recently crossed over. His message was so loving and profound it moved me to tears. I knew then I was indeed connecting with spirit when I channeled.

I'm sharing the channeled message I received from the dog in the hopes it will bring comfort and reassurance to anyone who feels their pet is lost to them.

I connected to the dog in spirit and asked, "Are you okay?"

The dog answered, "Everything is beautifully, blissfully wonderful here. I am running, playing, and there are so many others to run and play with! Please tell her (the dog's owner) I didn't want to leave her so soon, but all the days we had together were magical. I fulfilled my soul contract with her. I came as a being of love. I loved her every day I got to be with her, and I know I will see her again.

"You must realize that I and other animals are spiritual beings. We are spiritual teachers. We are spiritual beings every bit as you are. The difference between animals and you humans is, we know we're all one. We're very aware that we're all connected and always will be. We come to bring balance to the Earth, families, and individuals energetically."

I then asked, "Can she [the dog's owner] connect with you?"

To which the dog replied, "We can be together any time that she closes her eyes, opens her heart, and intends that connection. Invite her to picture her most loving memory of us together and feel for me. I am always here for her."

The next question I asked the dog was, "Is there a reason you were together [the dog and his owner]?"

The dog responded, "I came to her as a healer and a teacher. I would change the energy in a room whenever I felt it needed it, just by wagging my tail. I would often come lay at her feet and encourage her to pat me, to initiate the healing process within her, to adjust her vibrational field, and raise her frequency so she could experience life on the level that she intended."

Next, I asked the dog, "Is there a special lesson you came to share?"

He eagerly replied, "Yes, the importance of playing, of reveling in this beautiful world. I loved to play in the water, to run and roll in the grass, embrace life, and to demonstrate it so strongly that she could not help but feel the same. The most important lesson I came to share as a spiritual teacher is to reside in the now moment, which is the only moment you actually have access to.

"While I was on the Earth plane, I did not speculate about what the next day might bring. I did not ruminate about my yesterdays. I never spent time like that, and I want her to recognize that her power is in the present, and to bring herself back to that whenever possible.

"Tell her it would be my greatest joy if she remembers me with a smile and her heart fills with love and to remember the happy memories of all the things I did to make her laugh. I did those things because when she laughs, it elevates her consciousness. And I know that is her mission—to raise consciousness.

"Prior to our coming together on the Earth plane, we were with the Noble Wise Ones who helped us pick paths for this life that would best suit our souls. I knew she was one who had come to help raise the collective consciousness for the grand awakening. I was in touch with her spirit guides; they connected with me and gave me nudges much in the way I would nudge her to relax, breathe, and take her attention away from all those never-ending thoughts racing through her brain. I nudged her to take time away from that, to just sit and breathe and be, and pat my head and look into my eyes to see the depths of love there.

"She would sit and look into my eyes and feel how much she loved me, not knowing that love was being sent right back to her magnified. This is a magical property we animals have: We not only absorb all the love from our caregivers, we amplify and return it to them. This is why it feels so fulfilling and warms your hearts so.

"In those moments, she knew that we were soulmates. I'm of her soul family, and we will be together again. Tell her there may come a time when you meet another who reminds you so much of me. It may well be me. I may look different, but there will be traits of my personality that will make you pause and take a second look and wonder if it is me, returned to you. But even if I come again, I will still be available to you here. That is the beauty of it all. Because like you, I am multidimensional. I can be here and be there at the same time."

I then told the dog, "She would like guidance about getting another dog."

The dog replied, "It makes me so happy your heart is still open to loving another, that our experience was so fulfilling that you want to re-create it. I wish to say, there are many dogs who are living in cages. Beautiful souls like rescue dogs waiting to rescue you. It is a two-way rescue. They rescue humans as much as they are rescued by them. If you visit a place like that, you may connect with a little puppy who has been abandoned, or you may meet an older one who's been returned because his owner could no longer keep him. You may meet one who has lived much longer than I did, who outlived his owner and is now there waiting, hoping to have another home. Keep your heart open to all the possibilities. You'll know when you meet another who reaches out and touches your heart. 'I miss you so! I want to leap into your arms and cover your face with kisses. This is such a wonderful visit for me! When I crossed over there were so many here, but I looked around for those who I knew, and I was lonely. But I very quickly made good friends here. This is such a wonderful feeling to connect with you. I love you so much. This is a happy day. I am a happy dog!'"

When we think of animal communication, we often think of connecting with our animals, whether alive or in the spirit realm. However, we can communicate with wild animals, too, as this next story illustrates.

One student had a lifelong terror of snakes. She even stopped her daily walks for a period of time because someone had reported to her seeing a snake in the wooded park near her house. The avoidance didn't work, because she started encountering snakes crossing through her yard or appearing on her porch.

Since she could not avoid them by avoiding her walks in wooded areas, she went back to her walks. One day, she met up with a very large gray snake stretching across the path ahead. The snake froze, and she froze until she had the presence of mind to slowly back up and go a different direction.

The next day when she arrived at the same spot where the snake had been, she asked to channel a message from the snake. The woman received a long message of love from him that began with him asking her to remember all the times she had seen snakes during her life. The snake reminded her that none of those snakes had ever coiled or even hissed at her. He clearly said, "Neither I, nor any of my kind, mean you harm." The woman felt such love from that snake that her lifelong fear of snakes dissolved immediately. She never again saw snakes around her house or in the woods.

CONNECTING AND COMMUNICATING WITH YOUR ANIMAL

The process of learning to communicate with animals is possible for everyone if it is your desire and intention. To begin, find a quiet place, close your eyes, and take some deep, conscious breaths. Move your awareness from your head down into your heart. Focus on the still, quiet place within your heart as you continue to breathe. Notice your heart expanding and filling with love. Continue to expand your heart until you feel love in every cell of your body.

Then, bring the presence of the animal that you would like to communicate with into your heart. See the animal in as much detail as possible. Next, either silently in your own mind or verbally out loud, ask the animal for permission to communicate with them. When you feel you have their permission, start communicating with them in a way that is lighthearted and open. If you feel any resistance or feel that you are not receiving communication, focus back into your heart and into the love that you have for the animal. Some animals might be shy or have a way of communicating that takes more time to understand or comprehend. Trust yourself and continue to stay in your heart and focus on love.

Once you begin to interact with the animal and have a connection, you might start expressing yourself to them and share with them your intention to communicate. When you are ready, you can move into asking them questions. Remember, you might receive their answer as an image, picture, physical sensation, or emotion. If possible, respond to them in the same way. For example, if you receive an image in your mind as a form of communication from the animal, respond to them by placing an image of your response in your own mind. As you practice, you might discover that it's very easy to communicate with animals when you slow down and focus your attention on your animal. Over time, you will increase trust and confidence in each other.

CHAPTER 17

MEDIUMSHIP AND RECONNECTING WITH LOVED ONES

Was the death of a loved one the catalyst that spawned your spiritual awakening or desire to communicate with the other side? For many people, the desire to reconnect with a deceased loved one, which might include a beloved pet, allows them to go beyond their limited beliefs about life and death and open up to more that is possible. It inspires one to ask the questions: Who am I? Where did we come from? Where will we go? Why am I here?

The same might be true for someone who has encountered a near-death experience or life-threatening disease that causes them to question their own mortality, purpose for being, or to become curious about what lies beyond. These events can lead to powerful desires to awaken, discover our truth, and a deeper truth in the world around us.

One of the most painful experiences for most people is the loss of a loved one. Another life-altering experience can be facing the real possibility that you yourself might die. Many people live in fear of dying or how they might die and never allow themselves to fully live. The fear of death and dying is one of the most common fears on Earth.

A dear friend and student came to the Art of Channeling after her son transitioned. She had gone to channels and mediums who had connected with her son. However, she wanted her own connection with her son. This is a recount of her experience: "The Art of Channeling course has completely changed every part of my life, *forever!* I wanted to learn to channel to connect with my son, to know that he was okay, and for him to know that I loved him. In one of my first daily journaling sessions I asked him for a message; one of the things I wrote was that his suicide had nothing to do with me. When I read that I felt certain I'd made it up, because of course that's what I wanted him to tell me. After all, I wasn't a REAL channel, just a mom wanting to connect with her son.

"Not long after that, as I was reading aloud a message that I thought was totally unrelated to my son, I *felt* him in the words so strongly. I just *knew* in my heart the message was from him. What I felt while reading those words brought up a memory from when my son was just a toddler—here was this adorable two-year-old describing some of his past lives—then he finished by saying, 'You were always my mom.' That forgotten memory is what opened my channel to allow me to trust myself and my channel. I'm more aware of his presence in my life now than ever before, and I absolutely know our connection extends far beyond this life experience.

"Having a personal connection with my son was my intention for taking the Art of Channeling. I had no idea that the relationship I would develop with my channel would be as significant as it has turned out to be. It has allowed me to know my Divinity, to know why I'm here, to realize my purpose, to come fully into my power, to know my worthiness, and to truly know that 'I am everything I wish to be, I already am.' My relationship with my channel is by far my most important relationship. I love and appreciate it just like a relationship with a best friend, because that's exactly what it is for me. I'm forever grateful to Sara for offering The Art of Channeling."

In my own experience, the shocking transition of my beloved brother was the catalyst to my own spiritual awakening journey. Some years later, my entire world was turned upside down when I was diagnosed with cancer at a young age. While I would never wish these things on anyone, I can see now how they were seemingly divinely orchestrated to help me to wake up, open to higher truth, discover my ability to channel, heal, and live my purpose.

Not only can these experiences awaken one on a deeper level, but they might also allow a person to move beyond the illusion of death. When one discovers the ability to connect with a loved one on the other side, proving without question that there is life after death, one begins to live with greater peace, ease, harmony, joy, and opens to a whole new world of possibility. Channeling is the amazing tool we have to transcend the illusion of death to live fully in the light of truth and love.

Some explain this phenomenon as mediumship. Mediumship is a common term used to describe a person who can tune in to and communicate with a being or loved one who has crossed over to the other side. You might even know of extraordinarily gifted mediums who have achieved great levels of fame and publicity for their ability to provide detailed information from those on the other side. This is a form of mediumship, but anyone can open up their awareness to communicate and receive messages from loved ones who have passed over.

Like other forms of channeling, there are many different ways in which someone might receive messages and communicate with a loved one on the other side. For many of my students, the easiest way is to use the automatic writing technique. You can use a similar technique as asking your soul what it wants you to know, but in this case, you would use your deceased loved one's name.

Begin by finding a quiet place, take out some paper and a pen, and then close your eyes and take some deep breaths. Invite in the presence of your loved one by thinking of a time when you loved them the most, did something fun together, or remember them being really happy. Focus on what they were wearing, the color of their hair and eyes, anything you remember about the location you were in, and other things that you saw, heard, felt, smelled, or even tasted. Allow yourself to feel their essence all around you and notice the awareness of their consciousness around you, beside you, or above you. You can enjoy this reconnection with them as long as you wish.

When you are ready, ask them what message they have for you. Then open your eyes and start writing whatever comes to you. Allow whatever messages you are hearing or thinking to flow through you onto your paper. Keep writing and don't worry about making sense of it or editing it. You might feel like you are making it up. That's quite normal. Keep going. Write until you feel their message to you is complete or you feel their energy recede.

This might be a few words, a few sentences, a few pages or more. It's perfectly fine to stop and take some deep breaths and ask again, "What do you want me to know?" Or you can ask, "What message do you have for me?" It doesn't matter how long or short the message. You might even feel an abrupt end to the message, which is also a normal occurrence. When the message is complete, read it back to yourself out loud.

For those who verbally channel or practice with a buddy, you might ask your buddy to guide you through this same process and then allow the answers to come through you verbally instead of through automatic writing. You might also use the Pyramid of Light process at the end of this chapter. It can be done simply through following the visualization process and then stopping to write what comes to you or something your buddy can guide you through.

One inspiring student, a woman from British Columbia, explains how her mediumship reconnected her to her son after his transition. "I came to the Sara Landon community on a path begun four years prior when my 32-year-old son left this physical realm as a result of a head-on car collision. The journey through the grief of my loss led me many places, from shock to finding peace through meditation, and from curiosity about mediumship to a love for all things related to elevating consciousness.

"When an acquaintance promised that Sara's Art of Channeling class would change my life, I registered to participate. I found the immersion in channeling community and finding a buddy were key elements to my success and ability to channel. Nobody could have been more gobsmacked than my buddy and I when we were invited to try verbal channeling. Much to my surprise, it actually happened! Imagine channeling the voices of the bear and lilacs, as well as a message from my soul about freedom. It was all recorded on Zoom.

"Now, a year later, my channeling buddy and I cherish our friendship and continue to meet to converse and exchange channeled messages on a consistent basis. Sometimes our channels overlap, or they have us both meeting on a playground as a metaphor for fun and creation. Although we could not have ever predicted it, we now both use our gifts to channel messages of wisdom and healing for the upliftment of others.

"Channeling is a passion that helps us to understand more of who we truly are. It is a world of expansion. I am a whole new person in the wake of it. My son is always with me and communicates with me constantly. He wants me to live out loud and assures me that my joy is linked to my regular connection to that place where he resides through channeling and mediumship. I need not ever fear the loss of this transcendent knowing that *he is with me.* I have found deep joy within my despair thanks to channeling."

Knowing that you can reconnect with a loved one on the other side at any moment is one of the most life-changing opportunities that channeling presents to you. It is a natural and normal experience that you never intended to forget. It will allow you to move beyond the illusion of death. When you discover the ability to connect with a loved one on the other side, proving without question that there is life after death, you will live with greater peace, ease, harmony, and joy, and a whole new world of possibility will open up to you.

THE PYRAMID OF LIGHT VISUALIZATION

Allow yourself to arrive deeply into this moment, where anything and everything is possible for you in your life, in your relationships, and in your creation of your reality, any way you wish it to be. The power of the Pyramid of Light to go to the place beyond, the place where your Higher Self, and the Higher Self of anyone and everyone, is always available to you. There is a reality, beyond what you experience in your limited human experiences, or beliefs in what's possible. From this place, you can connect with your own Higher Self, and the Soul and the Higher Self of anyone. As you do, that love, that reverence, and that harmony can be brought through from the higher planes into your physical experiences.

The Pyramid of Light is whatever you create it to be. As you project the holographic image into your force field of consciousness, you create a place of the light, in the light, the Pyramid of Light, where you can go to connect, to re-create, to restore all things back into light and back into love.

Take some deep, conscious breaths. If you are ready, it is time for you to go to your Pyramid of Light. As the path to your Pyramid of Light opens up, make your way toward it. You may find yourself floating through the air or dancing through the clouds or moving through a tunnel of light or traveling in an airplane or a jet or riding a unicorn. Find your way toward the Pyramid of Light.

You're on the path now; you're making your journey. Up ahead you can see it—there it is—you're almost there. Notice how you're traveling. Notice how you're getting to your Pyramid of Light. It can be any way that you wish it to be. So as you make your way to the Pyramid of Light, up ahead of you now, you can see it. You're getting closer and closer now. Notice where it is. Is it hovering up above the clouds? Is it on a mountaintop? Is it suspended in thin air above a beautiful ocean?

Wherever it is, make your way now. As you get closer and closer, what do you notice about the Pyramid of Light? How big is it? What color is it? As you get even closer and you now are walking the final steps to the Pyramid of Light, reach out your hand and touch the side of the pyramid. What do you notice about the pyramid? What do you notice about the makeup and the structure? Is it solid? Is it fluid? Is it holographic? Is it pure light that you can stick your hand through?

As you notice the door to enter the pyramid, what do you notice about the door? Is it a tunnel of light that opens to invite you in? Is it a square door or a round door? Whatever it is, make your way through the doorway and enter the Pyramid of Light. As you do, notice the grand structure. Notice the power of this Pyramid of Light. Notice how good it feels to come home to this Pyramid of Light. What do you notice around you? What do you notice about the inside? How tall is the pyramid? What are the walls made of? What do you notice about the floor that you're walking on?

As you're walking through the Pyramid of Light, make your way to the center of the pyramid into a very special sacred place. As you enter the center of the pyramid, is it a separate room? What do you notice? Is there a chair or pillows, or a beautiful rug? Are there tapestries? Are there beautiful gems and jewels and crystals adorning the center of the pyramid? Are there comfortable chairs, or is there a table? Or do you notice two beautiful cushions sitting together in the pyramid in the very center?

As you're now in the center of the pyramid, take a moment to fully embody your highest self, inviting in your soul, your Higher Self. Now moving into full embodiment of the god and the goddess that you are or the king or the queen. Invoking and embodying the royalty that you are, the power that you have. Coming into complete and total embodiment of your soul or your Higher Self, you may find your body transforming into more light, higher frequency, higher vibration, feeling pure love flow through your entire body. Fully embody your power. Inviting in your Ascended Master self, feeling yourself fully in your mastery as the Alchemist of Light that you are.

As you are ready, there is someone here, someone moving toward the Pyramid of Light who is coming here to meet with you. Who is it that is making their way to the Pyramid of Light? It can be anyone—a family member, a friend, a lover, a business associate, someone whose relationship with you may have been a struggle, or maybe you felt they left their incarnation too soon. It can be anyone who has ever lived throughout all of history, currently in body or in nonphysical form. It can be an Ascended Master; it can be an Archangel.

Who is it that is here? As they make their way into the pyramid, notice that they are now walking toward you, coming to meet you in the center of the pyramid. What do you notice about them? What do you notice about what they're wearing? They're getting closer and closer now; you can see them clearly. What are they wearing? Do they have shoes on their feet? And if so, what do they look like? What does their hair look like? What does their structure look like?

As they now make their way into the center of the pyramid, look deeply into their eyes. What do you notice about their eyes? As you focus upon their eyes, now they, too, are embodying their master self, their Higher Self, their soul, the truth of who they are. They are now fully allowing the god or the goddess within to be embodied by them. As they fully come into the embodiment of their Higher Self, what do you notice about them? What do they look like?

As you greet each other, as the masters that you are, experiencing each other as the embodiment of the higher selves that are the truth of you, make your way to a comfortable seated position, looking across at one another. You may be sitting at a table or comfortable chairs or on beautiful pillows seated perfectly in the center of the pyramid. Find your way into a comfortable seated position.

What is it that you would like to say to them? Say it now. Say it out loud. Tell them what you want them to know. Then what is it that they have come here to the Pyramid of Light to say to you? Let them say it now. What is it that you would like to ask them? Ask them now. What is it that they would like to say to you to answer your question? Let them say it now. What is it that they would like to say to you? Let them say it now.

Is there anything else that you would like to say to them? Say it now. What else would they like to say to you? Let yourself hear it now. If there is anything unresolved or unsaid between the two of you, let it be known here in the Pyramid of Light that there is only love. The truth of you is that there is only love and that the truth of them is that there is only love.

Now either together or using your own power, let anything between you that is not of love be given to the Light—release it, bless it, let it go. Let anything that is not of love be released in the Light, consumed in the Light; illuminate it in the Light and allow it now to completely reemerge into the Light and be re-created from the highest truth that there is only love. Now that all things are restored to love, to truth to peace and harmony, are there any final words that they would like to say to you? Are there any final words that you would like to say to them?

Now it is time for them to leave the Pyramid of Light. You may choose to bless them and wish them on their way. You may wish to embrace them, hug them, and kiss them. Maybe you shake hands for a job well done. As you say your good-byes now, they are moving from the center of the Pyramid of Light, making their way out of the pyramid. Notice whether they are floating or walking.

As they make their way out of the Pyramid of Light, you can see them floating or walking. Getting even farther in the distance now. Moving fully into the Light. So that all you see in the distance now is Light. They have made their way back into the Light as you stand in the center of your Pyramid of Light, fully embodying your power, your truth, and your radiance. Fully allowing yourself to receive the love and the Light that is here for you.

This is the power of the Pyramid of Light. It is always here for you. It is always available to you. You can bring forth the Higher Self of anyone and meet them here. You have the power within you to return all things to LIGHT and love. You have the power to go here and have the conversations you wish to have from the highest levels of truth, aligned to the soul of you and the soul of anyone you choose to meet here in the Pyramid of Light.

Take a deep breath. It is done. All is complete. You are one in your wholeness and your completeness. There is only love. Take another deep breath, and when you are ready, focus yourself back into this moment. Back into the room that you're in, the chair you may be sitting on. Feel your body supported in the chair. Feel your feet on the ground. Wiggle your fingers. Wiggle your toes. Beautiful, and so it is.

CHAPTER 18

THE HEALING POWER OF CHANNELING

Channeling might possibly be the greatest tool we have to heal physically, emotionally, spiritually, and mentally. I have witnessed some of the most profound and miraculous healings through channeling. In my own experience, channeling has healed every ailment and issue in my body with no formal medical assistance or treatment. It has provided me emotional and spiritual healing simply through the unconditional love, acceptance, and compassion expressed in the channeled messages that I receive.

Channeling is essentially the modality used for healing or services performed by a healer, like Reiki, craniosacral, body work, therapeutic touch, and many other types of healing. When referring to healing, it usually references one who is opening their own channel to higher vibrations, frequencies, and Source Energy that naturally allows healing to occur. Some healers channel messages from the body or feel energy in a place on one's body where they are directed to move their hands or awareness to facilitate and support the healing process.

The very process of channeling requires one to raise your consciousness and vibration. This immediately allows one's body to move out of resistance and into peace and well-being as one summons Source Energy through the elevation of your frequency and consciousness. This allows a person's physical body to heal, transform, and regenerate.

It also allows a person to elevate their consciousness and frequency to heal mentally, emotionally, or spiritually. When one raises one's consciousness, you begin to see things in a new light and from a higher perspective. This elevation of consciousness through channeling can show someone a different, more evolved view of what might have once been an emotionally disturbing experience or memory.

Channeling also allows a person to heal from deep emotional grief experienced by the death of a loved one. It helps one to remember that death is not the end, but a transition into a higher state of consciousness not limited to the physical body. While I have met many students struggling with the grief of losing a loved one, one particular student stands out most to me.

I first heard her story and witnessed her deeply emotional grief on a community call for one of my courses. She was sharing with the community how her son had very recently died at 18 years old in a tragic accident. Her pain was almost unbearable to witness. She was viscerally struggling to get through the day-to-day activities of life and questioning her own desire to go on. Despite the compassion I felt from her, I had never witnessed such grief and wondered if she would ever find peace.

Our community supported her, and she became a part of my Masters Class program. She immersed herself in The Council's messages and the teachings of how to integrate them in her own life, especially as it related to overcoming her grief. She joined The Art of Channeling to communicate with her deceased son. My community and I have watched firsthand as she has opened her own connection to reconnect with him and channel messages from him directly that have healed her grief and suffering.

Before long, I saw her grief transform into love and her loss transform into an even deeper connection with her son on the other side. She is now writing a book with her son about their journey together in life and beyond. I will never forget when shortly after taking The Art of Channeling, I heard her explain how she is now channeling messages for other bereaved mothers from their children on the other side. I will forever be inspired, uplifted, and filled with unconditional love by her courage, strength, resilience, as well as the miraculous healing and transformation that occurred.

Here is her story: "When Sara shared with the community that she was writing a book on channeling, I contemplated with inquisitive curiosity what the 'art of channeling' truly means to me. First, I would like to share why learning to channel is personally sacrosanct at this crossroads in my life, while recognizing the ultimate motivator that drives my desire to master channeling today. I am a bereaved mother whose only 18-year-old miracle child transitioned into spirit in a hiking accident on Kauai a little over a year ago, only three weeks after my own mother's passing.

"Immediately following the death of his physical body, I was enraptured with a deep knowing that learning how to expand my relationship with my son to where he presently exists in spirit was now my single most important Earthly focus. Our almost 19 years together on this planet were absolute Heaven on Earth, characterized by glorious unconditional love for each other, acceptance of everyone we encountered, divine connection during extensive travels with diverse peoples around the world, rich learnings exploring universal truths, adventurous fun with copious giggly laughter, and abundant soulful experiences.

"My son and I are soulmates, likely twin souls, who continue to masterfully live our lives together in the adventure of a lifetime. Over the past year, I have developed a profound life-altering understanding through channeling in meditation and automatic writings that prior to our magnificent life here on Earth, we had previously agreed as spirits in our soul contract to this highly vibrational, richly rewarding yet deeply challenging life journey ahead. In each present moment, I am delightfully aware of my son's awe-inspiring infinite essence in my every breath.

"My human mother's heart still yearns for my 'angel boy' to remain contained within his beautiful human body that I birthed into this world. Simultaneously, however, my expansive eternal soul is also acutely aware of the divine blessings since his transition—a life that is filled to the brim with his clever and creative signs, flowing interconnectivity with poignant synchronicities, guiding sparks of pure magic, and his brilliantly orchestrated miracles every day.

"Learning to connect with my son in spirit through opening my clear channel to his current realm of wisdom has been paramount to my healing and spectacular for me and everyone around me to witness. I am beyond grateful for Sara in my life. With genuine love and abiding support from Sara and her amazing community, I have advanced my ability to consistently connect with my son and channel him, while remembering who I am, who he is, and who we all are—divine radiant light beings housed inside these miraculous human vessels.

"My heavenly Earth connection with my son has miraculously continued since his passing without interruption, timeless without end, and I know that he walks alongside me in spirit each day. Love continues to emanate outward from us into this world, and our elegantly entwined radiance and exquisitely blended energies continue to shine through me. I've come to understand through Sara and the Council's teachings that we are all channels with an ability as humans to conjointly expand the relationships with our loved ones in spirit, as we thrive in joy and happiness with them by our side for the remainder of our lives on Earth.

"While healing from the very real, painful yet beautiful, human emotions of grief, we can magically transition and transform ourselves to allow the flow of infinite divine wisdom, other-worldly ethereal love, and the everlasting life force of our loved ones in spirit that ultimately change us forever through deepening our connections using the transcendent and enduring art of channeling."

One of the most painful experiences for most people is the loss of a loved one, especially a child. Over the years, I have been in awe of the healing that occurs when one learns how to reconnect with one's departed loved ones now on the other side. The healing powers of channeling are available to everyone as each person individually opens their own channel to higher wisdom and their loved ones on the other side.

Many of my students have also begun channeling messages both intentionally and sometimes spontaneously for others. These messages are allowing those around them to also receive the healing benefits that channeling has to offer. Here is a story about how channeling can offer the gift of deep emotional healing to others in your life.

One of my students, a brilliant man from California, had a profound and extraordinary experience during a meditation when the presence of a young woman materialized to him. The young woman was the sister of a dear friend, who had passed away unexpectedly during the middle of the night some years prior. The night of the woman's passing, her brother was asleep in the other room. He was awakened by a loud unusual noise, but thought nothing of it and went back to sleep.

The next morning, the brother discovered that his sister had died in the night. Unable to call for help, she flung her cell phone against the wall, which was the loud unusual noise. The brother was devastated, overcome with guilt, and blamed himself for his sister's death.

It was during this meditation that the deceased sister, now on the other side, connected to my student. She asked to have a message conveyed to her brother that his guilt was unfounded, that his actions or inactions were not to be blamed. The student wondered how he could possibly approach his friend and say, "Your sister, whom I have never met, has a message for you. She wants you to find joy and release yourself from this self-imposed burden of her death. There was never a choice you could have made that would have altered her fate."

When the message was delivered, the brother felt the release of guilt; he found the strength to forgive himself and to embrace the truth that no alternative choice would have altered the outcome. With gratitude he admitted that the passage of time had failed to ease his burden, but this sacred message, delivered with love and understanding, had unveiled a path toward healing.

The healing that occurs through channeling is remarkable, life-changing, and truly inspiring. Anything and everything truly is possible as you reconnect to your own unique connection to Source Energy and higher wisdom. Some people come to channeling as a form of healing, while many others discover the power it has to heal simply through the consciousness and vibration it offers. There is no doubt in my mind that channeling has the power to heal each one of us and quite possibly, heal our world.

The final story I will share with you might surprise you and best illustrate how channeling can bring light to even the darkest places on Earth. One of the most inspiring stories I've ever heard from one of my students was from a woman who was working as a psychiatrist treating violent patients within the prison system. She had been attempting to apply evidence-based medicine in the treatment of two particular mentally ill patients with little to no success. After participating in The Art of Channeling, she decided to toss everything aside that she typically applied and channel for the two violent patients.

The first patient had not only committed violent crimes for which he was in prison, he had also been raped while in prison. She told him that she was going to channel for him a different perspective on who he was and what he had done. He agreed and she began to channel. Although she cannot remember exactly what she said, the message that came through her was of love, forgiveness, how worthy he was, how it was understood that the things that he had done were not the truth of him but as a result of the pain and suffering he experienced in lower consciousness, and to know that from the highest realms he was loved. When she opened her eyes, he was crying and expressed his deep appreciation. From that moment, she shares that he has not been violent to anyone in any way.

She wondered if it would work on another violent patient who had been in the prison system for over 42 years. Again, she told him, "We are going to try something different today," and she started to channel for him. When she opened her eyes, he was different and something within him had shifted. He admitted to her everything he had done in his life, which he had never admitted to anyone. A new door had been opened to his heart that had never been opened before, as he himself had been a victim of violence and abuse starting at a very young age.

Hearing her story was one of the precious moments that I will remember for my entire life. It reminds me of the power we each have to not only remember the truth of who we are, but to see others for the truth of who they are. In this case, to see the Divine within another despite the violent criminal that the world has deemed these two men to be.

I believe the ultimate healers are truth and love. Opening your channel has the ability to bring love and light to places you could never possibly imagine. If you will allow it, you will be used as a miracle for others in ways that you could never comprehend. You can bring light, love, and truth to the places that need it most and see the miraculous power to heal even the deepest pain, trauma, and suffering.

A Final Message from The Council on Divine Love

We are so pleased and delighted to have the opportunity to speak with you on this fine and glorious day indeed. You are everything you wish to be, you already are. You are a Steward of Divine Love in the world. You are so much more powerful than you could ever know. Your purpose for being, your purpose for being here in a body, is to love, is to have fun, and to experience great joy.

You knew when you came into this experience that not all moments would be perfect joy. You knew that there would be a range of emotions that you would experience in your time here. You knew that some days would be joyful and fun, while others would be full of grief and struggle. But you were not afraid.

You are a courageous being. You knew your own strength. You knew your own power. You came forth knowing that you could overcome anything that you endured in this human experience. You are courageous, and you knew that you could overcome it all because you are a Divine Being. You knew that. You knew that you were here for the fun of it, for the joy of it, and for everything else that came along with it.

The sadness, the grief, and the struggle you have experienced in your life has served you. It has taught you great love. It has taught you great compassion. It has taught you how to feel. That is very important. It has broken you open. That is a wonderful thing.

There is not any experience that you will undergo as a human that is ever wasted. Each moment serves, each experience teaches, each experience helps you go deeper into the remembrance of who you are. The only purpose, the only reason, is to remember the Divine Being that looks out beyond your eyes, that is connected to all things, that is powerful beyond words. You are a Steward for Divine Love, because Divine Love is *what you are*. It is what you came here to bring to others, to humanity, and to yourself.

Love of self is the greatest thing that you can achieve. If you can learn, Dear One, to love yourself, to truly, truly love yourself, then you will find the peace that you desire. You will find the love that you desire in your life. You will find the harmony in all things. You will foster great bonds with other humans and with the nonphysical guides and beings that are always available to you.

It is a feeling of worthiness that eventually gives you the permission to allow all of this into your life. Once you know your infinite worth, once you know how important you are, everything becomes available to you. Everything begins to show up the way you have dreamed it to be. Your greatest desires will unfold for you, but it is on the other side of this wall that you have put up around your heart. You must take down the wall so that *you* may really, truly feel the love that you are. That is your power.

You are Divine Love. You are the force of love in the world. And the only thing that's holding you back is fully allowing your own love to be realized by you. From there, you invite in everything to your experience. You invite in the love that you desire so deeply with another. You allow in the bonds and the connections with humanity. You invite in the forces of all things to support you. There is a great ease with allowing in all the support that is here for you to guide you, to show you the way. It is a wonderful thing.

As you go forth in your day, *remember* that you are the steward of Divine Love in the world. We are always with you. We are always available to you. You are everything you wish to be. You already are. It is all within you and it always will be. We love you, we love you, we love you. And with that, we are complete.

CONCLUSION

YOUR NEW EXTRAORDINARY LIFE

This is not the end of *You Are a Channel*; it is the beginning of your new extraordinary life. It is the beginning of a calmer, happier, more peaceful experience within you that will transform the world around you. It is the perfect time for you to fully step into being all that you are. This entire journey has been divinely orchestrated for you to come into the realization of the truth of who you are and all that is here and available to you.

Many people experience profound and life-changing transformations as a result of channeling and discovering their own ability to channel higher wisdom and connect with their souls, angels, and guides. It's common for you to notice changes in your relationships, circumstances, perspectives, desires, and so much more. I hope this book inspires you to discover your greater calling and more importantly, live your life to the fullest. You now have the ability to tap into infinite wisdom anytime you wish and in any and all situations.

Trust yourself and trust everything that is happening for you. Trust that you will receive everything that you need and more. You have drawn this book to you in divine right time, for the perfect unfolding of your destiny as a channel of Divine Love and Light in the world. Let the perfect next step come to you. Follow the energy and allow the light of higher consciousness to guide the way forward. Let it be easy, effortless, harmonious, and fun!

When you feel yourself in resistance, trying to figure things out, struggling to trust, or in a state of overwhelm, take three deep breaths and go from your head into your heart. Then, come back into the now moment and reconnect to Source Energy and higher wisdom. All your power is in this now moment. Then ask the question, "What does my soul or my angels and guides want me to know?" Stay open and allow higher wisdom to come to you and guide you on your path.

Have fun with all of this—play, laugh, create, explore, and imagine the possibilities. Allow yourself to integrate the higher wisdom you receive, day by day, in the most enjoyable ways for you. And most of all, be gentle with yourself.

Embrace your newly discovered gifts and abilities. You might find that you express yourself more fully in your daily life. Play and have fun and be fully open to all that you are. It is going to be so beyond what you can even imagine as you allow yourself into levels of consciousness that you have never experienced in physical form before. You are everything you wish to be. You already are. It is all within you and it always has been.

This is a book you will want to read repeatedly and refer to frequently on your channeling journey. While some things might not apply to you now, the expanded awareness you received in this book might attract new, exciting abilities and potentials to you. Allow the magic of this magnificent adventure. Live fully, love fully, and be all that you are. Remember, you are The Council here on Earth, and your life is meant to be so, so very good for you.

15 HELPFUL TIPS FOR LEARNING TO CHANNEL

1. Commit to a Journaling and Automatic Writing Practice

- Close your eyes, drop into your heart, and take three deep breaths.

- Ask: "What does my soul want me to know?"

- Open your eyes and just start writing whatever you hear and feel.

- *Important:* Read your journaling out loud or have someone read it back to you. You can also record yourself reading it.

2. Channeling Is a Lifestyle

- Make time for it; commit to it; be devoted to it each day.

- Approach it like your relationship with your best friend.

- Your higher self/channel should be like a deep, intimate relationship.

3. Give It Permission

- Ask yourself if you are ready to give your channel full permission to come through.

- The process of fully allowing and giving permission may take time.
- Be gentle on yourself, and when you are ready, give permission.
- Common barriers to giving permission: Not wanting to be weird, being afraid, being concerned what others will think, and fearing rejection.

4. Trust, Trust, Trust!

- Trust yourself even when it seems random, too easy, or like you're making it up.
- *You are NOT making it up!*
- Trust that your connection will always be there.
- Balance being impeccable with trust.

5. Everyone's Way Is Unique

- Don't compare yourself to anyone else!
- However it comes through is perfect and will always expand and evolve.
- As you practice, it will be clearer and easier.

6. Most Important Is YOU Living It

- Channeling is 100 percent for you, first and foremost.
- *Living it is the very best part!*
- Every message is also for you as it comes through you.
- Apply the wisdom and tools to change and transform your life.

7. The Channel Has No Judgment

- Get in to channel through seeing others as pure love.
- When in channel, you experience no judgment, no right/wrong from the channel.

- You might notice judgment in your own mind, and you might also notice that the channeled information is not coming through as judgmental.

- Higher perspective is offered without fear, judgment, or limitation.

- Feel a sense of innocence and oneness.

8. Being a Conscious Channel

- You are translating streams of consciousness.

- It's normal to be conscious and aware while channeling.

- Let your mind step aside and drop into your heart.

9. We/Us and Me/I

- It's normal for the channel to communicate in plural tense such as "we" or "us" versus how you might normally speak or write using the term "I" or "me."

- Sometimes the channel may come through and the energy feels like a collective.

- It's also normal to feel like it is your higher self or soul coming through you versus a collective or guide.

- Many people channel their higher selves and guides at different times.

10. Protect Yourself by Filling Yourself Up with *All* of You

- There is only love.

- *There's nothing you need to protect yourself from!*

- No energy is outside of you or overtaking you.

- There are no dark forces when you are in a state of love.

11. Higher Self, Collectives, Animals, Light Language, Mediumship, Art, and Music

- There are endless forms of channeling for you to explore.

- Your channeled connection can express through you in many ways, so be open to discovering new modalities.

- Use love as a powerful tool to help you open your channel and connect with loved ones.

- Focus on going from your head to your heart and connecting through your heart as you open to a higher consciousness.

12. Water, Rest, and Play

- Drink lots of water.

- Honor your body and rest when you need it.

- *Play and have fun with it!*

13. Using Trigger Words and Phrases

- The channel often starts the same way. For example: *Welcome, welcome, welcome.*

- You can use phrases to help you get into the channel. For example: *You are everything you wish to be; you already are.*

- Consider a mantra to help you open your channel.

- Example: Pure bliss, pure bliss, pure bliss.

14. Guides, Archangels, and Ascended Masters

- Be aware that it is natural and normal for guides, angels, and ascended masters to "show up" and then recede over time.

- You aren't doing anything wrong if your guides appear to recede.

- You might be guided to information, words, experiences like a scavenger hunt.

- Explore what you are guided to with curiosity and openness.

- If you feel the presence of a guide, archangel, or ascended master, ask them to tell you their name. You might then research the name given, if you are unfamiliar with them.

- Not all guides will offer a name, which means it's not necessary or could be distracting.

- Guides appear to help you and support you when you need it.

- Be open to new guidance as you expand your channeling.

15. There Are Many Different Ways to Experience Channeling

- Use all your senses to activate channeled connection.

- See, smell, touch, hear, taste, feel, think.

- Spirit can use all your senses to bring you messages.

- Focus your senses to connect with Spirit.

GLOSSARY

A

Animal Communication

When someone transmits or translates a message from an animal, living pet, deceased pet, bird, dolphin, whale, or some form of animal species. Communication between human and animal can often result in understanding an animal's desires, perspective, or feelings, and can also cause some kind of change or improvement in the animal's situation or behavior when understood. *For more on animal communication, see Chapter 16 (page 135).*

Automatic writing

A writing process used to receive guidance and messages from one's soul, higher self, guides, loved ones on the other side, or from one's higher consciousness rather than from one's own conscious mind. It allows a person to produce written words without consciously writing them, or writing that is produced involuntarily when the person's attention is seemingly not directed to an expected result.

C

Channeling

The act of connecting, communicating, and communing with higher wisdom and beings in higher dimensions of consciousness. *For more on different types of channeling, including trance, verbal, nature spirit, and psychic channeling, see Chapter 3, page 19.*

Councils

Celestial beings of higher consciousness who organize to connect and communicate with the intention of assisting humanity on its journey.

The Council

A collective of ascended master beings with a higher level of consciousness and a grander perspective of the human experience.

Creator

The pure conscious of Source from which we came and will return, the essence and energy of the Divine within.

Creator frequency

The frequency of the *I Am* from which we came from and will return, the frequency of all Creation.

D

Dimensions

Levels of consciousness available through the raising or lowering of one's vibrational frequency that offer unique variations of experience. The 3rd Dimension is the dimension of separation; the 4th Dimension is the dimension of transformation; and the 5th Dimension is the dimension of pure love.

G

Galactic Collectives and Galactic Beings

Beings and collectives that exist in higher dimensions of consciousness beyond the Earth experience and often assist humanity in its evolutionary awakening.

Great Awakening

The global event of becoming aware that there is more to you, life, others, and existence.

Guides

Guides are often beings who have advanced beyond the need to incarnate on Earth and now assist and guide humans from the other side. Their intention is to help souls to attain their highest potential and self-realization on Earth.

H

Heaven on Earth

A state of consciousness where one realizes the peace, harmony, joy, love, abundance, well-being, freedom, and beauty within.

Higher Self

One's own energy and higher consciousness connected to the source of all existence and the Divine within.

Higher Wisdom

The awareness of every experience of every lifetime: past, present, future, and eternal.

L

Light Language

Light Language is a cosmic language known and understood by the soul, but uncommon to any language on earth. It is accompanied by sound and energy to convey messages. *For more on Light Language, see Chapter 15 (page 127).*

M

Mediumship

Mediumship is when a person specifically channels a loved one or specific person now on the other side either for themselves or as a medium for another person to communicate with someone on the other side. *For more on mediumship, see Chapter 17 (page 143).*

N

New Earth

Refers to the ascension of humanity and/or an individual into the 5th Dimension of pure love, bringing new opportunities to create a better life and a better world for all.

Q

Quantum Healing Hypnosis Technique

A form of hypnosis created by Dolores Cannon designed to help people access the Somnambulistic state of trance. QHHT is a powerful tool to access the all-knowing part of one's self often referred to as the soul, higher self and guides, collectives, and councils.

S

Source and Source Energy

The source of All That Is, the energy and consciousness that created everything, the source of all existence from where you came from and will return.

Star Families and Star Beings

See: *Galactic Collectives and Galactic Beings.*

V

Visualization

The formulation of a mental image, object, situation, or experience on one's mind or higher consciousness.

W

Wayshower

A human who is incarnated on Earth to show the way to awakening to higher consciousness and self-realization.

ACKNOWLEDGMENTS

To my students: You are the inspiration for this book. You have inspired me beyond words with your perseverance, devotion, and courage to live your truth, overcome your fears, and share your gift of channeling with others. I am deeply touched and forever changed by all that you have taught me. You have brought more joy and love into my life than I ever thought possible. I wish for each of you to know what a bright light you are in this world. You will empower, inspire, and uplift others around you and contribute to making a positive impact in our awakening world. Follow your heart, trust yourself, and shine brightly! I love you all.

ABOUT THE AUTHOR

Sara Landon is a globally celebrated transformational leader, spiritual teacher, and channel of The Council. She has been called the leader of leaders for the next generation of teachers, wayshowers, channels, coaches, and guides who are contributing to raising the consciousness and vibration on the planet at this time. Sara is the best-selling author of two books: *The Wisdom of The Council: Channeled Messages for Living Your Purpose,* and *The Dream, The Journey, Eternity and God: Channeled Answers to Life's Deepest Questions,* co-authored with *New York Times* best-selling author Mike Dooley.

As the voice of The Council, Sara's intention is to be the purest channel of their wisdom and teachings, which offer a grander perspective of what is possible for each of us—and our beloved human family—as we elevate our consciousness to new levels. She focuses herself, as the ultimate student, to live the wisdom and teachings at the highest level, and is dedicated to helping others discover that they, too, have the ability to connect to these greater levels of awareness and guidance.

A powerful luminary, Sara's greatest joy is helping those who are ready to play in new levels of energy to reconnect with *all that they are*, so they may live, love, and lead in this time of awakening. Sara holds the vision of a fully awakened world, where all beings co-exist harmoniously with one another and Earth. Through numerous courses, coaching groups, and activations as well as her widely celebrated Global Masters Class program, she has helped thousands of masters from around the world integrate the wisdom of The Council and create profound life-changing, long-lasting realization.

For more information and resources, please visit: **saralandon.com.**

Hay House Titles of Related Interest

YOU CAN HEAL YOUR LIFE, the movie,
starring Louise Hay & Friends
(available as an online streaming video)
www.hayhouse.com/louise-movie

THE SHIFT, the movie,
starring Dr. Wayne W. Dyer
(available as an online streaming video)
www.hayhouse.com/the-shift-movie

***

*THE GOLDEN FUTURE: What to Expect and How to Reach the Fifth
Dimension,* by Diana Cooper

PSYCHIC NAVIGATOR: Harnessing Your Inner Guidance, by John Holland

*THE GUARDIAN GATEWAY: Working with Unicorns, Dragons, Angels,
Tree Spirits, and Other Spiritual Guardians,* by Kim Wilborn

*SPIRIT TALKER: Indigenous Stories and Teachings from a Mi'kmaq
Psychic Medium,* by Shawn Leonard

All of the above are available at your local bookstore,
or may be ordered by contacting Hay House (see next page).

***

We hope you enjoyed this Hay House book. If you'd like to receive our online catalog featuring additional information on Hay House books and products, or if you'd like to find out more about the Hay Foundation, please contact:

Hay House LLC, P.O. Box 5100, Carlsbad, CA 92018-5100
(760) 431-7695 or (800) 654-5126
www.hayhouse.com® • www.hayfoundation.org

———

Published in Australia by:
Hay House Australia Publishing Pty Ltd
18/36 Ralph St., Alexandria NSW 2015
Phone: +61 (02) 9669 4299
www.hayhouse.com.au

Published in the United Kingdom by:
Hay House UK Ltd
The Sixth Floor, Watson House,
54 Baker Street, London W1U 7BU
Phone: +44 (0) 203 927 7290
www.hayhouse.co.uk

Published in India by:
Hay House Publishers (India) Pvt Ltd
Muskaan Complex, Plot No. 3,
B-2, Vasant Kunj, New Delhi 110 070
Phone: +91 11 41761620
www.hayhouse.co.in

———

<u>Access New Knowledge.
Anytime. Anywhere.</u>

Learn and evolve at your own pace
with the world's leading experts.

www.hayhouseU.com